MOODIE'S BOY

GROWING UP IN AFRICA

Peri Mika Chinoda

Printed in the United States of America

Library of Congress Control Number: 2020906553
ISBN: Softcover   978-1-64376-986-8
            eBook   978-1-64376-985-1

Republished by: PageTurner Press and Media LLC
Publication Date: 04/15/2020

To order copies of this book, contact:

PageTurner Press and Media
Phone: 1-888-447-9651
order@pageturner.us
www.pageturner.us

Contents

This book is dedicated to the late Minnah Pigot-Moodie and Canon Edward Chipunza, my late parents, my family and siblings, and all those facing obstacles in their pursuit of education.

Chapter 1

The young man who would be his father was a handsome, round-faced, broad shouldered, energetic and of medium built. Although he did not always comb his hair, he kept it short and clean of dust and dirt particles from the fields and the environment as a whole. He dressed in clean loincloth and always carried with him a bow and arrows, and sometimes an axe was hanged on his left shoulder. A few years earlier, he had been initiated into adulthood in accordance with the traditional African custom. Boys aged twelve and thirteen would be taken to an isolated and remote area and spent three or four days for an experience similar to "boot camp". There they would be circumcised and taught ways and responsibilities of adulthood and fatherhood. After a few years, he was now of marriageable age.

In the same village, lived a girl (*musikana*) who would be his mother. She was in her mid-teens and was a shining star of the village. Many boys and girls of her age envied her bodily and facial features and light skin complexion. She was slightly tall and skinny with almost over-sized but sharp-pointed breasts. Traditionally, the size of these breasts was an obvious asset in her marriage, particularly in tender moments with her future husband and in nursing her babies. Her family was highly reputable in the village and had taught her the roles of womanhood and motherhood within the context of marriage.

Nyemudzai and Tasiwei had known each other since they were children, and when that acquaintance developed into publicly noticed mutual love; he shared his intentions with his uncle and aunt. On a pre-arranged day, he followed the local girls to fetch some water from the river. Nyemudzai summoned his courage and sweet-talked Tasiwei into lagging behind other girls by a few yards. Then he stretched out his hand in front of her and offered her a beautiful, tender and green leaf he had just plucked from a nearby shrub. He did not have to say a word. She knew what that meant. She looked at it. She looked at him.

Without saying a word in turn, she violently knocked the leaf off his hand to the ground and picked her pace to catch up with the other girls. Did she really mean to reject his proposal or was she playing hard to get, a usual practice in the village? On his sixth attempt in nine months, she accepted his proposal. For engagement, he gave her a locally threaded necklace. She in turn gave him nduma (a girl's personal effect). *Nduma* could be a home made necklace, bangle, or ring. Sometimes one's personal piece of cloth would be accepted as nduma.

The two were a perfect match, and it seemed they were made for each other. Who would have waited much longer before marrying such a beautiful and much respected girl? But he committed a terrible offense in the village by making her pregnant before giving *roora/lobola* (brideprice) to her father, as the traditional custom required. He did not have the necessary resources for roora. His father, Komechi, had died when he was just a child. The herd of cattle and a few personal possessions his father left had been taken over by his uncle who inherited his mother to become his second wife. Thus Nyemudzai had no choice but to become a migrant worker in the gold mines of the neighboring country of South Africa.

After two years, he returned with enough money to buy cattle and exchange them as roora for his lovely wife. So when all the traditional marriage negotiations and formalities had been completed, the village elder pronounced the two now married. But that was not all that was required for a marriage to be official in a land that was now controlled by white man's laws. The Europeans had by this time completed the colonization process of his ancestors' land and had named the country Rhodesia, after the British colonial and business tycoon, Cecil John Rhodes. Thus, the two still had to be married by a Native Commissioner, a white man's government official, in the eastern District of Melsetter. The bride and bridegroom walked for two days to the nearest Native Commissioner's Office.

The white man's colonial laws categorized traditional African first names as heathen and required all Africans to abandon such names and adopt European ones. The bride and bridegroom knew that the Native Commissioner in charge of marriage registration would not accept his given name, Nyemudzai, and hers, Tasiwei. After much thought and name searching, he named himself Simon and she named herself Jay. Thus, these names became their passport to being married in accordance with the white man's laws. They started a beautiful and lovely home, but traditionally, the marriage status was still incomplete.

Men of Simon's caliber and status had to structure their families in accordance with the customs of their society at the time. They were expected to have large families of two or three wives and several children. These would provide more labor and produce more food. Thus when his material resources dwindled, he decided to return to South Africa and work in the gold mines. Upon his return from his second expedition, he made arrangements to marry a second wife. After complying with the new laws, he married Sekwi.

It was the beginning of the rainy season in what was then the British colony of Rhodesia. It was just six months after Simon's return from his third work expedition in the South African gold mines. It was time for him to reestablish his authority, which had been the responsibility of his first wife, Jay, while he was away. His third wife to be had not been brought to him yet. Each time he returned from South Africa, he purchased several head of cattle, and fathers who had teen daughters would approach him with offers. They would hope to have him as a son-in-law. By the local standards, a man who had been to South Africa was rich. He was a gaisa (a recent and wealthy arrival from the South) that many younger men envied. He became a role model, and many young men followed his footsteps.

Like his grandfather and father, Simon was a renowned hunter in his own village and the surrounding villages. His grandfather was a prince in the Zimuto kingship and a well-known hunter. He decided to break away from the loyalty and pursue his hunting career. He followed herds of elephants for about a hundred miles or so up the Save River. Using traditional weapons, he killed many elephants and sold their tusks to the Portuguese traders from the coastal areas of the Indian Ocean. Through barter trading with these traders, he obtained and learned to use a rifle. It was the same gun that Simon's father inherited and was in turn passed on to his son when he died. Even though Simon did not inherit anything else from his father, this rifle proved to be worth more than gold in his later life.

However, the colonial laws declared it illegal for an African to possess and use a gun of any type. The Africans viewed this prohibition as political and oppression. They resented what they regarded as unjust, oppressive and discriminatory laws. After all the Europeans were allowed to own and use firearms at will. In fact, the government organized and sponsored sharp shooting lessons for them. Thus, it became a common practice among Africans that whenever someone acquired a gun, it became a community's closely guarded secret.

With this rifle, Simon killed many animals such as kudus, antelopes, springboks, zebras, wild hogs, and elands. He fed and supported his family through hunting, and gained fame, friendship and potential in-laws throughout the region. He was a gaisa, and even though he had been away during those years he was in South Africa, in the eyes of the villagers he was still an expert hunter possessed by his ancestors' spirit of hunting (*shavi*). Thus it was not difficult for him to acquire a significant social status and reclaim the respect of both the young and the old, and even the local political authority.

After three months of his third return from the "South", he decided to throw a party. There was no need to send out formal invitations. A general announcement passed from village to village by word of mouth was sufficient. The weather was perfect for such a party, slightly hot and windy, and the kind of temperature people were accustomed to. Around mid-afternoon, people from the surrounding villages started arriving in large numbers. They came partly to admire this new gaisa and partly to feast on beef and game meat served with the traditional *sadza* (thickened corn meal and mush) and African beer. After the formal introductions of the village hierarchy, which was boring and a waste of time to many people, Simon stood up in his elegant and colorful outfit and addressed the people.

"To the Honorable chief of the village, and to the chiefs of other surrounding villages," Simon bellowed while clapping his hands with fingers tightly close to each other to produce a loud sound, as was the custom. He had a very strong and loud voice so much that there were echoes from the nearby cliffs.

"To my beloved mother and to my lovely wives and to all of you who have honored me by coming to this party, I say welcome. I thank you all for coming and taking care of my family while I was away all those three years. It is a great feeling to come home and be with my people—("—*Yeeeh, taura mwana wedu*"), "speak, our child!" some from the audience interrupted. He waved his hands and shook his body as if in ecstasy, the women ululated, and men clapped their hands and whistled. Those with musical horns produced loud sounds in warm welcome. He stomped his feet in the form of traditional dance to acknowledge their response. A row of women stood up in waves, and started dancing around and fanning him with their shawls. Highly elated, he sat down to a deafening sound of applause and whistling.

After the harvest, he sent his best friend to negotiate roora/lobola (bride price) with Chemwaita's parents. She was a virgin girl of sixteen years, light skinned, slightly round faced, with big ears, and of medium height and weight. She walked with a bouncing step as if to pronounce the shaking of her succulent and well-pointed breasts. Her parents were proud of her for being well behaved and respected in the village. Indeed, her beauty and dedication to hard work made her the star of the family, and no man would have hesitated to offer any quantity or amount of roora/lobola for such a girl.

When her father asked for a plough, two oxen, and four cows, a set of clothes for her mother, as well as continuously steady supply of fresh game whenever possible, Simon's marriage negotiator did not hesitate to agree. This was a fair exchange and a "thank you" token for such a beautiful wife. He was not buying her; that was not the custom. The underlying concept of roora/lobola, after all was to give something to the bride's father in appreciation for the proper raising of his daughter. Of course, raising a child was a communal activity, and the mother in particular did much of the work as far as raising a female child was concerned. Nevertheless, the family structure was basically patriarchal, and it was the father who had the first and final say in such family matters.

Simon had done the same thing to marry his two wives, and they had already made him what he was now. They had given birth to several of his children. The first one had born him four healthy boys, Mwaitangei (Mwaita, for short), Chomunoda (Chomu), Azviperi (Peri), and Tangai. Sekwi had born him a girl, Verina and a boy, Efias. Every man preferred his wife or wives to give birth to more boys and fewer girls. Simon had five boys already. So he willingly gave the required roora/lobola to Chemwaita's father. Within days Chemwaita was escorted to Simon's home and became his third wife.

She had to be housed in the first wife's house for several weeks before she could move into her own house, as was the custom. A temporary cottage was built for her to move in and start her own family. Somehow word went around that she was a virgin, and many people, including the teenage boys in the village, were curious to see some physical and emotional signs of her first encounter with a man. Everybody, including some older women and men, were watchful. The boys decided to use Simon's older child as an observer and informant. So when the night came for him to share a bed with her for the first time, Jay made the necessary arrangements and escorted Chemwaita into the hut where Simon was waiting for her. Word of this expected encounter had already spread like bush fire among the village people who were fond of gossiping. For several weeks after Chemwaita had been made into a woman, there was laughter all over the village. Some people, especially teenagers, joked about it and even mimicked and dramatized the sounds and bodily movements of the encounter itself as if they were witnesses.

Although polygamy was a normal and accepted traditional practice, quarrels and disputes were common and normal feature in most polygamous families. Wives engaged in serious and fierce competition to gain more favor from the husband, and children were often caught in between vicious physical and verbal fights. Village courts were always overcrowded with numerous family cases having to do with jealousy, and they used an array and variety of social sanctions to deal with them. But no matter how serious a case and squabbles were, no divorce was granted. In this traditional social structure and set up, divorce only came up in cases involving witchcraft.

Simon's household was no exception to problems involving jealousy. With his three wives, children, cattle, goats, and chickens all in place as well as fields to do peasant farming, it was now time to consolidate. It was time to expand and carve his niche in society. It was time to raise a family (or rather families?). The women had their roles to play in the household. He was the boss and everything had to be done according to his word. Everybody had to respect him and even fear him. The wives could not dare express their jealousy over each other. The children had their roles to play in the household and had to respect the mothers. In fact, the rule was for all the children to regard each one of his wives as a mother. They had to address each one as "amaiguru" (elder mother) or "amainini" (younger mother) depending on her seniority in that marriage. The penalty for causing trouble due to jealousy was heavy. The woman could be beaten or reported to her family or worse, taken to the village court. The child could also be beaten or denied food for a day or so. Other privileges could also be withdrawn. A mother of the child who acted up and was suspected of doing so on behalf of his/her mother, could also be punished together with the child concerned. So tranquility was maintained that way. A man worthy of that word was supposed to run his family with a heavy hand, and Simon did just that.

Food was cooked simultaneously and served to the husband at the dare (a place, usually under a tree, where men and older boys sat and had their meals) or in his cottage. The boys from each wife's house would bring the food to their father. If a woman had no children, then she would bring the food herself. Thus, the skills in cooking determined which food was eaten or favored by the husband. Often poorly cooked food or unappetizing food was given to the younger boys or the dogs.

"I hate Amainini Sekwi. She is such a bad cook," said Chomu. "We always end up being given that food, I end up going hungry," he whispered aside.

"What did you say?" his father said.

Mwaita looked at Chomu. Chomu looked on the ground trembling with fear. He knew he was in trouble for saying that against one of the mothers. The penalty for saying that was unthinkable. He did not know what to say.

"No-no-nothing," he stammered, visibly shaking. Everybody stopped eating. There was dead silence except for noise from a cock chasing a hen to mate and distant voices from the kitchen nearby.

"You should never say that again, you hear!" his father threatened. "You must finish that sadza alone, you hear," he bellowed. The voices in the kitchen stopped suddenly. Everybody was still frozen from fear.

"Yes, Baba. I'm sorry. I will not say that again," Chomu promised. Nobody took that incident lightly. It was a serious offense against one of his wives, and everybody knew the consequences.

Simon's first wife was always unhappy to hear that her children were being fed that type of food. However, she would not dare say anything about it. She only devised a plan. She set aside her well cooked sadza, *nyama* (meat) and *muriwo* (vegetable relish). When her boys brought back dirty wooden plates and bowls from the dare, she would give them the food. They were to eat it quietly and never to say a word to any one about this plan. That was the only way for her three older boys to survive that ordeal.

Chapter 2

"Wake up; its time to drive cattle to the dip tank," Simon yelled at his two older boys. "Mwaita! I say wake up or I will get in there and whip you," he roared.

"Okay, father, we are up," Chomu answered in an attempt to avoid provoking his father's anger.

The boys got out of the kitchen where they always slept. The moonless night was still pitch dark. Stars were shining brightly. It must have been three or four o'clock. Yet these boys, the oldest barely twelve years old, must drive twenty heads of cattle to and from a dip tank more than seventeen miles away. The law of the country clearly stipulated that every cattle owner must bring them to be dipped in an oblong pool treated with a pesticide; otherwise they would die from parasites or spread other infectious diseases.

The younger one of the boys, Peri, who must have been four years old, had to help his brothers going to the dip tank. He was a bit too young for this, but every child had to start that early taking such responsibilities in the family. Of course, his older brothers would take care of him. They would shelter him against the usual boys' fights, against pushing and shoving that went with many people fighting for first positions in dipping their cattle. A lot of the times they would take left over sadza and beans with them to eat on their way back home as the trip took the whole day. On their way back home, Mwaita and Chomu decided to wander in the woods looking for wild fruits, berries and just having fun. They wove their way in between some undergrowths and thick grass, while Peri was trailing way behind them.

"I have been bitten, I have been bitten! Help me, help me, brother!" Peri screamed while shaking his right leg. His brothers, who were far ahead of him and occupied with some attractions in the woods, could not hear his cries. They kept on going and talking between themselves.

"Brother Mwaita, please help me! I have been bitten by a snake!" Peri screamed and shouted repeatedly. After several screams, the two boys heard his cries and rushed back to where he was sitting down and rubbing the spot between two smallest toes on his left leg.

"What happened? A snake bit you? Where did it bite you? Where did it go?" Mwaita frantically kept on firing questions at his brother.

"Oh, Mai! What shall we do brother Mwaita?" asked Chomu in tears. "Is Peri going to die?" He asked again while stamping his feet on the ground in distress. In between chokes and fading voice, Peri managed to describe the snake as being small and slightly orange with a brown head. He said he did not see where it had gone. His brothers had disturbed the snake and perhaps in self-defense it had bitten Peri, who was trailing his older brothers. Upon feeling the pain from the bite, Peri had suddenly jumped and only managed to get a glimpse of the snake disappearing in the grass. There was no way they could figure out what kind of snake it was or where it had gone from that description. Within a few minutes, their brother fainted. He fell to the ground and soon was unconscious.

"Chomu, stay here with him. I am going to call Mom and Dad," Mwaita ordered. "But, I'm afraid! Please, don't leave us here alone, brother! Don't leave us!" Chomu pleaded with tears streaming down his cheeks.

"Okay, then you run home and call them. I will stay here with him," his brother impatiently suggested.

Chomu raced three miles as fast as he could. Upon hearing the bad news, Simon, who was just getting back from a hunting trip, threw to the ground the dead male springbok he was carrying on his shoulders. He quickly hid the gun in the nearest barn and instructed one of his wives to call the traditional medicine *man* (nyanga). He rushed to where Chomu left his two brothers. When he got there, he found Peri awkwardly lying on the ground with eyes closed and a very faint and undetectable heartbeat. Mwaita was crying in fear that his brother might be dead. Simon simply picked the unconscious boy up without asking Mwaita any questions and carried him back home.

A tall, skinny and long-faced traditional doctor dressed in heavy locally woven clothes and hat decorated with feathers was sitting on the wooden stool outside Jay's kitchen ready for action. He carefully examined the young boy's body and the spot where the snake had bitten him. He made three or four incisions, applied a concoction of *muti* (traditional medicine) on it and wrapped the foot in old pieces of cloth. He mixed another type of muti in water and forced it down Peri's throat. He treated the young boy for three days and, on the fourth; Peri slowly began to regain his consciousness and be able to talk and eat by himself. Within the following week, he fully recovered from the snakebite, but developed a terrible phobia of snakes.

Another task that Simon's household had to perform was working in the fields. A child, usually a boy, would lead oxen pulling a plough, and help with cultivating fields or weeding. It was a task that started very early in the morning and lasted way into the day. While adults were busy working in the fields, younger children would guard the fields against wild animals. Hogs, baboons, and monkeys would descend upon the fields and devour the almost ready corn and other crops. Sometimes birds would also prey upon the staple food grains—millet, wheat, and rapoko. It was while chasing a full-grown male baboon that Peri had a scare of his life. The baboon suddenly turned and started chasing him with a deep loud noise. Peri ran very fast screaming for help. The tables were turned; the chaser became the "chased".

For health care Simon relied wholly on the local traditional healers. He had to because there were no hospitals or clinics nearby. The nearest clinic was at Biriwiri, twenty miles away. Walking to and from that place with a sick patient was a last resort. So for minor pains and headaches, local herbs and roots were used. Even children were educated on which root or herb cured which ailment. If a child was gradually losing weight, dry herbs were grounded into extra fine powder using flat sides of two small rocks. A skilled adult would load some of the powder into a short piece of dry reed. One or two adults would hold the child down while the tip of the reed containing powder was carefully and gently inserted inside the child's anus and the powder blown into it. That way, it was felt the child would not suffer from *mhepo* (bad air), as a result of intestinal worms or parasites such as tropical water-borne bilharzias. Most children were terribly embarrassed by this process. Besides, they hated traditional medicine because it had a bad taste. The way some of the untrained adults administered the medicine also contributed to the children's distaste.

The period soon after harvest, when all the grains were secured in barns, was a time of relaxation, fellowship and fun for both adults and children. Simon decided to have a beer drinking party at his home. Close relatives and friends were invited to enjoy traditionally brewed African beer while sitting in the cool breeze of the afternoon and the shade of a nearby big tree. While the party was going on and was at its peak, Tamboonei, Simon's brother, who was nursing some kind of headache, decided to ground some medicine on a grindstone to treat it. Peri thought the medicine powder was intended for him and decided to run away and hide in a cave nearby.

The party degenerated into a pandemonium and a commotion resulted as people feared for the missing child and started looking for him everywhere without success. He heard voices of the people looking for him, and the voice of his mother crying, but remained hidden, all in fear of the medicine. He only got out and sneaked into the house when the fear of the night and snakes overpowered that of medicine. He received a severe beating for disturbing the peace, worrying adults and for fearing some medicine.

Chapter 3

THE local traditional midwives delivered Simon's first five children by his first wife. The traditional medicine man or woman administered prenatal care. The same applied to the first three children of his second wife and two of his third wife. There were no complications, and all the children were healthy and strong. The problem was to surface later when a record of or some kind of information about these births was required. Simon, his wives and any of the responsible midwives were illiterate and would most likely not remember when these children were born.

For almost two years, Simon had succeeded in consolidating his family's status in the community. He had three wives, healthy children, fields with fertile soil and several domestic animals. People envied him in his community. He had selected a good spot to build a home. There was a river nearby with flowing fresh water. If he needed to hunt, he could do so in the surrounding woodland, which had duikers, rock rabbits, and bigger game animals such as elands. Indeed, the soil gave him what he needed for his family, and he was content. Everybody envied him.

This is the world he had created for himself and his household, but there was another world out there and he knew it since he had been to South Africa. The clothes he had brought with him from South Africa had all gone and he did not have any income to buy more clothes. In fact even if he had the money, there were no stores nearby. The ploughs and hoes he was using on the fields were all worn out. There was no way to replace all these. Because he lived so far away from the dip tank, sometimes his cattle could not be taken there for dip. Most of them started dying of diseases.

For two successive years, there was drought in the whole of Rhodesia. Simon's region was hit harder because it was isolated and separated from the surrounding regions by Mountains with high cliffs. There was no means of communicating with the outside world. Thus when the soil became unproductive because of the drought, starvation descended upon this area of the country with no means of relief from anywhere. There was no choice but to go to other surrounding areas and beg for food or work in other people's fields in exchange for corn, rupoko (local grain) or whatever agricultural products were available in that region. This was the responsibility of the women. The men stayed at home waiting for their wives to come back with food.

Most women had learned to develop survival social and economic skills. As a little girl, Jay learned pottery and basketry and was now skilled in making earthen pots and weaving baskets. She used these for barter trading during the period of scarcity. An interested customer could fill either a pot or basket with grains once or twice, depending on the bargain or the type of the grains. The two would then exchange their products, and the sale was completed.

Usually the women took their older children with them on food expeditions. These children helped the mothers by either carrying some of the food supplies on their heads or baby siblings on their backs. Many of those trips involved spending several days walking back to their villages. Sometimes they would feed on part of their supplies on the way back home so that by the time they arrived back home, they would have very little left. Within a few days, the food would run out again, and it would be time to go back and trade, beg or work for more supplies. These expeditions were very hard on the children, and they hated them, especially the begging for and carrying of food supplies.

When the children were at home, they performed household chores and looked after cattle and goats. They played various games, including hide-and-seek, chasing and *tsoro* (a form of checkers using four rows of small and shallow holes on the ground). In line with cultural practices, boys played separately from girls. This helped to ensure that there was no "hanky panky" among older boys and girls. They were all expected to be virgins until marriage, and it was a disgrace for one to lose virginity before that.

On many occasions, the boys violates territorial boundaries and invaded the area where girls often played. One of the areas they invaded was a shallow spot in Muroti River. Girls of various ages enjoyed swimming or just taking a bath in the river behind some rocks and shrubs. They laid their clothes on the nearby rocks, joyfully dived into the water and just had fun. Out of curiosity, the older boys would often stealthily walk to the spot to have a peep at the naked girls. They would tease the girls, snatch their clothes and run away with them. The girls would get out of the water and chase the boys to retrieve their clothes. As they did that they would further expose their naked bodies. Out of frustration, some of the girls screamed and others even cried, and the boys became ecstatic with laughter and enjoyment. The practice soon became a favorite entertainment for the boys, but a nuisance in the village.

When the situation seemed like it was getting out of control, the mothers of the village decided to do something about it. They appointed a strong and fast-running woman and assigned her the responsibility of dealing with the nuisance. She connived with the girls, and on a pre-arranged day, accompanied them to the river. She took off her clothes and hid behind a nearby shrub. As usual the girls got undressed, dived into the water and began to giggle loudly and just make some noise to attract the boys' attention.

Consistent with their previous practice, the boys stealthily rushed in, announced their presence by teasing the girls and snatching their clothes. Expecting the girls to get out of the water and chase them, they started running away. Instead they experienced the shock of their lives when they noticed a completely nude woman, wearing a mask, emerging from behind a shrub. She started chasing them. They dropped the girls' clothes and ran faster for their lives. She caught up with three ringleaders of the group, one at a time. Holding each one by the neck, she forcefully drew his face very close her exposed genitals. While vigorously shaking the boy's head she shouted, "You bad boy! Come on! Open your eyes. Is this what you want to see? Look at it then! Look, look! Do you see it? Are you now satisfied? Yeah? Yeah? Leave the girls alone, you hear?" The three boys were visibly trembling, terrified and humiliated. The younger boys fled in all directions, some were crying loudly. The girls, who had now emerged from the water to watch and enjoy the drama, were delighted and filled with laughter. The women's strategy worked and brought the whole problem to a sudden halt. For days, the boys teased each other about whose mother she might have been.

As Simon's family grew in size, the situation became extremely desperate. As his children grew up, there was now the need for education. There was no school nearby. The closest was about thirty miles away; not within reach of his growing children. His family could manage without going to the clinic, local and traditional medicine could be used instead. He could manage without professional midwives. For some time he could live without buying any supplies for his family because local provisions were available from working on the soil. But there was no substitute for schooling. Simon and all his wives had never been to school. Nobody had taught them to read and write. Even when he went to work in the South African gold mines, he depended on an interpreter to communicate with his Boer (descendent of the Dutch) employers who treated their employees more or less like they were slaves. He was not the only one illiterate anyway. There were other migrant workers from South Africa's neighboring countries of Portuguese East Africa (now Mozambique), South West Africa (Namibia), and Southern Rhodesia (Zimbabwe). Although they were all paid minimum wages, it was better than having no money at all. So his illiteracy was not much of a problem. He had learned to manage without being able to read or write.

The world was no longer the same anymore. The good old days had gone by. His children, especially, needed to learn to read and write if they were to live a different type of life from his. Social changes were now inevitable. When Jay took her two oldest male children to work for food at an irrigation scheme settlement, Nyanyadzi, or at an area near Rusitu Mission Station, the world began to open up for his children. They now knew there was another world out there where people lived better lives and the children were literate. When they went back home, they immediately began to show their discontent. They started sharing with the other children in the family what they had observed out there. Jay and the other wives began to show signs of being unhappy with the welfare of their children. Each mother started fending for her own children to the best of her ability. Members of a polygamous household, who were once at peace with one another and were united, started to think and act in different ways. A wall that once kept this region isolated from the surrounding regions began to crack.

"I am going to run away from here one of these days. Did you see how Tapiwa lives in Nyanyadzi? Why is life like this for us around here? Why don't we move and live near Rusitu Mission where there is a lot of food? That way we wouldn't have to carry food supplies like this?" Mwaita thought to himself. "Hey, Peri, you know what? I saw a car and a bicycle, and, ooh! A lot of strange things in Nyanyadzi," Mwaita added. "You need to go and see these things for yourself, Peri. You would be surprised to see what is in other areas," he continued. "I am tired of herding these cattle and goats, of being out here in the rain and of just being this much different from other children in other regions. I am going to ask mother to allow me to go to school. If she refuses, I am going to run away," Mwaita said with determination.

Mwaita was the oldest boy, now long past the starting age for school. He was going to speak out on behalf of the other children, at least of his own brothers, Chomu, Peri, and Tangai. The next day he decided to talk to his father.

"Baba (father), I want to go to school," Mwaita said looking at his father but avoiding eye contact.

"No, you cannot go to school. I need you to help me around here, herding cattle and protecting goats from leopards and guarding the fields against many wild baboons and monkeys. Besides, I never went to school myself, but still was able to go and work in South Africa three times. Your mother never went to school either but can make pots and baskets. What do you want to go to school for?" His father asked while carving a hoe handle. "I do not have the money to pay for school. You also need to remember that there is no school nearby. Mhakwe School is very far away from here. The point is you cannot go to school. So don't even think about it," his father concluded angrily. The same kind of answer and response was given to any other child who asked to be allowed to go to school.

To Mwaita war was declared. He was determined to pursue the matter this time with his mother or else simply run away from home. He would be sure to convince his brothers first that they also needed to go to school. When he confronted his mother with the idea, he was surprised to find out that she had been thinking along the same lines. Jay had decided that if her husband remained adamant against the children going to school, she would take unilateral action to ensure that her children would become educated.

During her expeditions to beg and work for food supplies at Nyanyadzi Irrigation Scheme and Dzingire, near Rusitu Mission, she had made some contacts with other women. She had raised the possibilities of her children being employed by some of the families on a part-time basis. Her idea was that her children could attend school in the morning part of the day and work in the afternoon. That way, they could work for accommodation, fees and books. When necessary, she would also come and work in their fields, and, some of her wages or food would be credited towards the children's school expenses or supplement their accommodation.

When Mwaita talked to his mother, this was the idea they agreed to pursue. They would do it even without Simon's approval. It would be a risk worth taking for all her children. She would defend them against the wrath of their father. One day Jay gathered all her four boys and discussed with them the importance of education and her secret plans to send them to an area where they would start attending school. All four boys jumped with excitement, and the fear was they would divulge the idea to other children and thereby foil the plan. She made them swear not to discuss the plan with anyone, and to be prepared when the time came to go away from home. During her expedition to Nyanyadzi to work and beg for food, Jay finalized the plan with one of the sympathetic families. Since there was no record of the birth of all her children, each would have to create a date acceptable to school authorities and declare it his birthday.

Mwaita, being the oldest, was the first one to disappear from home. He was employed by Mr. and Mrs. Bangwayo, and started attending school during the mid-1950s. When her husband frantically looked for him, she told him the truth. To override Simon on anything was a very serious crime; to execute a secret plan behind his back was a crime punishable by death.

"What is this? Who do you think you are in this family? You have no right to do that! He is my child, not yours. You are just an outsider here. I went through all the formalities and even gave your parents *roora*. I did all that not to give you permission to rule over my house," he went on and on. "I will return you to your parents for that and demand back everything I gave them to marry you!" Simon was furious and threatening all the way.

He carried out his threats by taking the case to the local village court. The village elders summoned Jay's parents to inform them of their daughter's offense and to attend the court hearing. After examining both sides of the case, Jay was found guilty of acting behind her husband's back. She was asked to apologize to her husband and to her father for disgracing him. In addition, she was fined six big pots of traditional beer, a goat, and two cocks. These would be killed and eaten at the time the village people would be called by Simon to drink the beer. As for Mwaita's fate, the elders of the village ruled that he should be allowed to continue attending school where he was. After all, they said, Simon would eventually benefit from his education. He marked their words that he would benefit from his children's education. That was the catch phrase. So he let the whole plan go.

After two years had gone by, Jay arranged for Chomu to follow in the footsteps of his brother. He left home and was employed by another family, which owned acreage in Nyanyadzi Irrigation Scheme. He made up his own birth date and enrolled in school. Very early in the morning before going to school, he would work on the acres, attend classes for five hours and work again after school for the remainder of the day. His wages would be withheld to defray food and accommodation expenses. The little that was left would be for clothes and school expenses. His mother would also come and work on the acreage to help with expenses incurred by the caretaker family. That was how the two boys managed to attend school.

The plan worked for a while until the school's demand and that of the employers became unbearable for the young boys. The boys would come back home complaining about the abuse that they were experiencing at the hands of the employers. They would explain why it was difficult to do well in school under such exploitative conditions. Jay decided to go and see the missionaries at Rusitu Mission. She had been told that they sometimes helped children with such financial problems.

"*Munodei, Amai?* (Literally: What do you want, Mother? 'Mother' is used here to respectfully address a woman who has had children)", Miss Donna, a husky missionary from Canada, asked with a Shona accent. Shona was the local language that was very close to Swahili.

"*Ndinochema nevana vangu, Mufundisi*" (Literally: "I am crying for my children, Reverend"), Jay said while kneeling and clapping her hands, a sign of deference. She had never talked face to face with a white person before, and therefore did not know how to address one. She had just started to crawl towards Miss Donna, with her face down, when Miss Donna said in broken Shona," *Isandipfugamirira zvayo, Amai* (You should not kneel and crawl for me, mother").

Mr. Merritt, another missionary who was more fluent in Shona, was called. The two missionaries stepped aside for a while for consultation. When they came back outside to where Jay was, they invited her into their kitchen. An African house girl (nanny) was called and asked to give Jay some food to eat. After a brief rest, she begged them for financial help for her children so they could attend school at the Mission's boarding school.

Jay was not the first one to come to the Mission for such help. People with sick relatives had always come to the Mission hospital for free medical services. Orphans had been bought there for care, and the poor had also been coming there to beg for food and accommodation. People in need of spiritual healing flocked there and found what they were looking for. Indeed, the Mission Station had become a true haven situated in the isolated and neglected part of the country. Providence had therefore inspired and led Jay to the right place.

Miss Donna gave her clean clothes to wear, replacing the rags she was wearing. She was shown where to take a bath. Jay was given a comfortable place to spend the night. The next day three missionaries called her to a room with furniture and decorations she had never seen before. Upon entering the room, Jay quickly sat on the floor. The missionaries persisted that she should sit in a chair. She wondered what the missionaries would say about her request.

Mr. Reeves, a one-armed missionary who was the most senior and very fluent in Shona, said, "*Zvakanaka, Amai, tichaedza kukubatsirai pavana venyu*" ("Its okay, we will try to help your children attend school"). The condition was that they would work for one of the missionaries on Saturdays and for two hours after school. If the boys did not raise enough money that way and the Mission's financial contribution was not enough; the parents would have to pay whatever was the balance. Jay reasoned within her that her children were already doing the same thing in Nyanyadzi anyway. Working at the Mission and going to school would not be any worse.

A two-day journey, on foot and with a baby on her back, was now worthy it. The deal had been struck. An opportunity for her children's education had been opened. The ancestors had opened the door for them, she thought. Her heart pounded faster with excitement and gladness as she rejoiced at the missionaries' offer. They gave her some money for bus fare back home.

Chapter 4

At the beginning of the following school year, Mwaita enrolled at Rusitu Mission to continue with his elementary education. Chomu remained in Nyanyadzi and was now joined by Peri, their third son.

"I want to go home; I miss my mother," Peri, now about nine years old, said to his brother. "This work is too hard for me, and I do not have enough time to sleep. They wake me up very early in the morning, when it is still dark. The boy called Tongai is mean to me and picks on me all the time. His parents do not do anything about it. I don't like it; I want to go back home," Peri went on and on complaining.

"Of course, work is always hard. You are not with your mother, so what do you expect?" his brother replied a bit irritated by Peri's complaints. Inwardly, Chomu was also unhappy. He was being mistreated as well and made to work more than was fair for a boy his age. He wished he would also go to Rusitu Mission where his other brother was now going to school, but he was still too young to be in a Boarding School. He would join Mwaita the following year. He knew that, but it seemed years away for him.

People from all over the country settled in the Nyanyadzi Irrigation Scheme area. The scheme was established for commercial purposes. Each family could own two to four acres and grew wheat, corn, tomatoes, vegetables, and fruits for sale. They were expected to grow enough to supply the whole country. At a time when machinery and technology was still in infancy, farmers relied on human hands to do the job. Everybody, including children, was expected to work on these acres. It was hard manual work, from dawn to dusk.

Such was the environment in which Peri was introduced. The Bangwayo family took him in at ten years of age. He was required to wake up at dawn, perform domestic duties first, and then of to school for five hours and come back and work on the acres until it got dark in the evening. This was the daily routine. Weekends were worse. A child hated Saturdays and Sundays when there was no school. School time became the only time to have a break from manual work.

When Chomu left for Rusitu Mission at the beginning of the following year, Peri remained in Nyanyadzi. Without his brother to turn to when the going got tough, he decided to quit work and school in the middle of the school year. Going back home was not an option for him. There was no chance for him attending school from home. Now that he had experienced school, dropping out was a very difficult decision to make. He could not manage working and attending night school at the same time.

"I am going to look for employment, work for the rest of this year, and save the money for school," Peri thought. It sounded like a good idea: work, save money and return to school, simple. A colored (colonial laws racial designation for a person of mixed blood) farmer, Maikiri, was looking for young boys to help take care of his farm on a full time basis. But before he could be employed, he had to have a junior employment registration certificate. In one day, he walked to the nearest Native Commissioner's Office twenty miles in a small town called Melsetter, now Chimanimani.

Samson, a youthful looking, short and dark-skinned African clerk in the Commissioner's Office, quizzed him on why he needed an employment registration card (ID) at that age instead of being in school. Samson also told Peri that the law required him to have a Christian first name for his registration. The headmaster, who had enrolled him in school in Nyanyadzi, had suggested that he be called Micah. He remembered that name now. So the name "Micah" and the words "Unknown Birth Date" were entered on his ID. Micah then became his official name.

Full time employment for boys of his age was only available on the nearby farms. The closest farm was owned by Mr. Maikiri. At the beginning of 1958, Micah, who looked thin and undernourished, and small but matured for his age, took up employment on Mr. Maikiri's farm. To honor his own pledge to save money for school, he asked his employer to withhold part of his wages and give it to him at the end of the year. Mr. Maikiri agreed, and it was a deal sealed. His employer seemed very nice. He gave all the boys working on his farm enough food, used clothes and blankets and allowed them spare time to play. As for Micah, everything was on track as he had planned. At the end of the year, he would get his money and go back to school. When the year ended, he took a bus to Melsetter where his employer lived. There he was to resign and get his money.

"What do you mean you want to terminate employment now? I thought you were to work for me for a long time," Mr. Maikiri angrily said. "You cannot leave now, go back to work, and that is final," he added and walked away.

Micah was astounded. He stood there frozen with his mouth open for what seemed to be an hour. What about his plan to go back to school at the beginning of the school year? He thought. His eyes started watering, and he started to shiver. What should he do now? He followed into the garage where Mr. Maikiri was repairing his tractor.

"Bu-bu-but I want to go back to school, Sir," Micah nervously stammered. "I told you at the beginning that I would have to leave for school at the end of this year, Sir," he added. Mr. Maikiri ignored him. "Sir, I want to go back to school. Give me my money you were withholding from my wages, and let me go," he said while crying.

The demand for money evoked Mr. Maikiri's anger. "What do you mean I have your money? What money are you talking about? I gave you food, clothes and your wages, that's it. I do not owe you anything. You can report it to the police, if you want. Where is your employment card (ID)? You are now fired!" Micah gave him the card, and Mr. Maikiri signed his name and scribbled a negative comment on it.

"Here, take your ID. Go away before I set my dogs on you," he threatened throwing it onto the floor, and walked out of the garage. As he was about to release his dogs from the cage, Micah quickly picked up his card, and took off sprinting and crying. He tripped and fell into a ditch. He got up quickly trembling with fear and sat up burying his face in folded arms resting on his drawn-up knees. He cried himself to sleep in that position.

When Micah woke up, it was now late in the afternoon. The sun was just about to set behind the surrounding mountains. There he was in Melsetter now without any money or employment. He did not know anybody in that town. It was too far to walk back home. Besides, there was no chance of attending school from home. He was now very hungry, thirsty and exhausted. He could not remember the last time he had a good meal. He did not know where he would sleep for the night or find something to eat. For a moment his mind went blank. Crying would not help him at this stage, he thought. Should he go to any home that he could find and beg for food and a place to sleep? At last, an idea came to mind. He remembered going to the Native Commissioner's Office for his employment registration card the year before. He remembered Samson, the clerk who issued him the card and asked him why he needed that card. Why not go to his office and ask for help in securing another employment?

The idea itself gave him wings and strength. He sprang up to his bare feet and, carrying his only possession of a pillowcase with an old pair of shorts and shirt, dashed to the Commissioner's Office. He barely made it there before the office workers closed and left for the day. Micah rushed straight to Samson's office.

"Excuse me, Sir. I am sorry to disturb you, but I . . . I. I need your help. Do you remember me? I came here for an employment registration card last year," Micah said with his head almost resting on his left shoulder.

"*Mufana* (Boy), what do you want? Do you think I can remember every person who comes here, yeah? Come on! Look at me! What do you want this time"? Samson said with an agitated voice. He must have had a long and bad day. Besides, it was almost time to get off work for the day.

"Please, Sir. Can you tell where I can find a job? I am looking for employment. I do not know anybody in this town, and my home is very far away from here. I do not have any money either. I beg you. Ndibetsereiwo mukuru wangu, ndapota (Please, help me, Sir. I beg you)," Micah was almost in tears when he said all this.

Samson stopped organizing files on his desk and looked at Micah from his head to his cracked bare feet for a long time, as if he was studying him. He said, "Come with me outside". Then he said,

"Do you see that house over there? Do you see it? Look through the branches of this big tree here? *Mufana uneluck sterik* (Corrupted Shona for 'Young boy, you are very lucky'). Miss Moodie's cook was here this morning looking for a young boy from the Portuguese East Africa (now Mozambique) to help in the kitchen and run some errands for him. Run over there. I don't think he has found someone to employ yet. Go now! Hurry! Goodbye and good luck!" Samson said hurriedly, for it was past time for him to close his office for the day.

Although he was tired and hungry, Micah ran as fast as he could. A couple of times he stumbled and fell. In his mind he was running a race against somebody. There was an invisible competitor. It was a question of do or die. Whoever got there first would win the race and get the job. It had to be him and no one else. That was his job. Nobody else mattered. Distance did not matter. Speed mattered. That theory of survival of the fittest and that instinct for self preservation overpowered him at this time. He got there within no time. While breathing heavily and sweating profusely, Micah knocked on the first door he came to. A dog came out barking. That scared him, and he felt like wetting his pants. He just stood there frozen with fear. Lucky enough, an African man was following closely behind and urging the dog he called "Popcorn", to stop barking or charging.

"Who are you? What do you want?" Jim asked with an unwelcoming voice.

"My name is Micah. I am looking for a job. I have been referred here by Samson, the clerk at the Native Commissioner's Office," Micah replied with suppressed fear and still almost out of breath. Sweat was still pouring out of his face and body. He was soaked wet.

"You speak Shona. Where are you from? You are not *Mupuka Wire*, are you?" Jim asked with some curiosity showing on his face. "Mupuka Wire" (wire jumper) was a derogatory term for an illegal immigrant worker from the neighboring Portuguese East Africa Colony now Mozambique.

"I am from Muroti, fifteen miles away from Mhakwe Primary School. I need employment, please," Micah repeated, as if Jim had not heard him the first time.

"Wait out here", Jim ordered and quickly disappeared into the house. Popcorn followed behind him.

Micah was called to come and stand outside the kitchen door, with only the top-half open. A European lady appeared and stood behind the bottom half of the door. She must have been in her early 70's. She was of medium height and weight. She did not look mean or threatening, as was the case with many Europeans in the country at the time. She studied Micah intensely, moving her eyes up and down Micah's small body without saying a word. Through an interpreter she asked, "Are you Southern Rhodesian? Where is your employment registration card?"

With a shaking hand, Micah reached into his shirt pocket and produced his card. It was partly wet from the sweat. He knew it had a negative comment on it from Mr. Maikiri. The thought of it brought a chill down his spine. He visibly trembled as Miss Moodie was examining the card. There was a long pause, a very long pause.

Apparently ignoring the negative comment, Miss Moodie broke the silence and said, "Micah? Is that your name?" A slight smile on her face assured Micah that there might be some good news coming.

Through an interpreter, she said, "Welcome. I want you to work for me. My brother George is in the hospital in Chipinge at the moment. But there is no problem. You will work here. The cook will tell you what to do. You can start tomorrow," she concluded. She was just about to disappear behind the door into another room, when she suddenly turned around and asked, "Where are your parents? Why are you not in school? Do they let you work?"

"A-a-a-a, they are at home," Micah stammered. "They do not have money to send me to school. Yes, Madam, they have allowed me to work," Micah said with some emphasis fearing that she might change her mind about employing him. She just nodded her head and went back into her dining room. Jim took Micah to the servant quarters, and gave him some food to eat. He showed him a room where he was going to sleep. That was to be his room in the compound, just like other African employees there.

Chapter 5

Minnah Sophia Pigot-Moodie was a British spinster. She and her brother Brigadier George Pigot-Moodie had fought for England in the Second World War. She was a nurse by profession. The two had moved to Southern Rhodesia, which was then a British Colony. They must have moved not long ago because in the storerooms, there were still heaps and heaps of unopened boxes and cartons. Their attitude and treatment of the African people was conspicuously different from those of the hard-core racist white Rhodesians. Their minds had not been polluted with racism and prejudice prevalent in this part of the world.

Minnah Moodie with "Popcorn"

From the look of their house and its contents as well as the size of their land, they were very rich. They owned two British-made vehicles chauffeured by two African drivers. In addition, they employed four other Africans as servants. Two were full-time garden boys (adult African males). To work in the kitchen and the whole house, they had two Africans whose experience would have enabled them to pass for a modern day professional cook and waiter. Africans were employed in large numbers on European owned farms and mines, and it was a common practice for Europeans to employ Africans to work in their households too. However, to employ six adult Africans to work in a household of two people was a luxury afforded only by the most-wealthy Europeans.

Servant quarters were comprised of two large rectangular buildings with flat asbestos roofs. Each building had one common shower and toilet. Married servants had two rooms each, while a single servant had one room. There was no provision for heating the water for a shower. Open-fire cooking was done outside the rooms. One could only cook inside when using a paraffin (kerosene) portable stove. No children were allowed at this compound. All married servants, except one without children, had their wives and children live in their rural homes. It was a common feature in the whole country to find the elderly men, women and children tending domestic animals (cattle and goats) and being in charge of peasant farming while able-bodied men were away working for the Europeans on commercial farms, in mines and urban homes.

The Africans employed by the Pigot-Moodies had considerably better conditions of service than most Africans employed elsewhere. They were paid higher wages and salaries, and sometimes got some tips from the Pigot-Moodies' British visitors. In addition, the servants were given adequate rations of cornmeal, beef, beans and salt. The cook and the waiter were issued a white uniform—long pants, jacket and apron and laundry soap. Drivers were given gray overcoats. Garden workers were not required to wear uniforms. All servants were given a small portion of land to grow their own vegetables, but could not keep chickens on the compound. For their health care, they went to the nearest clinic or hospital at the employers' expense. However, most of the servants relied heavily on African traditional medicine.

Micah was assigned a room and a small portion of gardening. Miss Moodie gave him a piece of paper with the order for his uniform and other provisions. He was malnourished, and needed some nutrition. He also needed some clothes and shoes; in fact, he had had only one pair of tennis shoes in his life. He could not believe his eyes when the store clerk gave him what Miss Moodie had ordered for him; two sets of khaki shorts, short-sleeved khaki shirt, white apron and laundry soap, and two pairs of tennis shoes. However, he still needed to ask for an advance in his salary so he could buy himself a blanket and a large mat to sleep on. He had slept on the floor all his life.

Micah also got his ration of corn meal, salt, dry beans and beef, but he had no pots and plates or other materials necessary for cooking. In fact, he had never had to cook for himself. For a child his age, the idea of cooking for himself was difficult to swallow. He no longer had a parent, a brother or older boys to help him cook, as had been the case before. He was now alone and had to fend for himself. Yes, he had to do something in order to survive.

Jim introduced Micah to Peter, the waiter, and showed him the kitchen. He gave Micah a description of his duties which included washing dishes, pots, and pans, carrying grocery from the store in a wheelbarrow. He was to make fire for the water heater and start fire in the kitchen stove very early in the morning. He had to make some early morning and afternoon tea for his employers including visitors. He was also expected to help Peter cleaning the rooms, making up beds and doing laundry. He would also help the cook as needed.

Both Jim and Peter were very nice and supportive to Micah. They trained him and were patient with him as he learned the culture of the White Man. The cook even allowed him to eat some of the old leftover food. Sometimes he left some food in the pots so that Micah would have something to eat. In this case, there was no need for him to cook for himself. Before long, Micah had gained some weight and looked healthier, except for the time when he was a baby feeding on his mother's milk. Traditionally, mothers were to breast feed their babies for more than eighteen months.

Peter was married, and he and his wife used one of the sections in the servant quarters. He was a Christian and a very religious man. He belonged to the Apostolic Faith and did not eat anything that had some ingredients of pork in it. When he had spare time in the kitchen or in between serving his employers' meals, he read his English Bible. He kept an English dictionary and a notebook nearby to look up and write down new vocabulary words. Daily, during his break time, he went to his room to pray. He prayed so loudly that other workers were annoyed and hated him for making such noise in the compound.

"Crrrrr, Amen!—Hallelujah,—Jesus Christ!—*Hosanna wekuDenga! Dzingai Mweya wakaipa paneni* (Jesus Christ, chase away evil spirits from me)," he would shout with a very loud voice. His wife would repeat similar phrases as well. This added insult to injury by increasing the level of annoyance.

Members of the African Traditional Religion in the compound accused Peter of attacking their ancestral spirits, which they believed interceded between them and God. Why would he label his ancestral spirits as being evil? After all Christianity, they argued, was a white man's religion that had made them effeminate and docile towards colonialism in that the Europeans came with a Bible in one hand and a gun in another. Besides, the Africans had another grievance against the white man's colonial laws that regarded their first names as heathen and demanded that they be substituted with Christian ones. Therefore, any African who converted to it was considered a traitor of his own culture and tradition.

The African Traditional Religion was based on a theological concept involving a hierarchical order of spiritual Beings. At the top existed God (*Mwari*), the Creator of all things (*Musikavanhu*) and the Most Powerful spiritual Being. Below God were the ancestral spirits who existed in hierarchical order. Worshipping God involved all these things. The worshipper simply asked, by name, the ancestral spirit at the lowest level of the ladder to pass the request to the one above him. The next one above would do the same and on and on until the request reached God. The worshipper could not and would not circumvent any one of these spirits, as they were vital intercessors between God and the people on earth.

That was why Peter was accused of wrongfully equating the ancestral spirits with evil. After all, God whom Christians believed in and Mwari whom Traditional Africans believed in were one and the same Being. The only difference was the approach, either through Jesus Christ in Christianity or through the ancestral spirits in the African Traditional Religion. Of course, some Traditional Africans believed in the existence of evil spirits, which tended to possess witches as they carried out their devilish ways in society. Perhaps these were what Peter was referring to in his prayers.

Jim, on the other hand, was a staunch follower of the Traditional Religion. He would also worship God privately and in accordance with the way his father taught him. He even knew some traditional medicinal herbs and roots. Many people working in the neighboring houses came to him for a supply of traditional medicine. This religious contrast between Peter and Jim caused some friction in the relationship between the two. The situation was worsened when it came to competition and seniority on the job. Junior workers were often caught in between this religious and power struggle.

Brigadier George Pigot-Moodie came back from the hospital feeling better but was looking pale and weak. He was tall and spoke with a very deep voice. He walked and looked at you with a military general's eye. His sister introduced Micah to him. He was very friendly and welcoming. After a few days, he walked in the yard directing and supervising the garden *boys*. Sometimes he took Micah to the garden to get some peas, green beans, carrots, tomatoes and other vegetables for lunch or supper (dinner).

Other times he rode his horses on the outskirts of the town and around the plot in a way that showed his battle skills. He must have been a great brigadier skillful in fighting on horseback. It was obvious that other Europeans in town respected him as a retired military man. Indeed he had his bedroom walls and hallways decorated with large pictures and paintings of the Second World War battles.

After four months of being at home, Brigadier George got sick again and was admitted into Chipinge Hospital. Everybody working for him felt very sad to see him get sick again. Within a month, word came that he had died. He was buried in the Melsetter cemetery, and his grave was covered with granite materials, a hallmark of wealth at that point in time. Miss Minnah Pigot-Moodie gave away some of his clothes to charity and others to her servants.

Chapter 6

Life seemed perfect for Micah at the Moodies' home. He had some new clothes, a better place to sleep and some food to eat. All his basic needs seemed to be taken care of better than ever before. The new cultural setting mesmerized him, and for a while did not know how to handle the change.

One day, when he was by himself cleaning one of the bathrooms, he decided to try using a modern toilet. He had never used a toilet with a seat. He was used to the pit latrine and to using bathroom in the bush with leaves for toilet paper. Thus, he did not know whether to sit or step on it and crouch. Micah did the latter and made a mess on the toilet and had to hurriedly clean it up before anybody could find out about it.

Using European materials was strictly forbidden. A servant was not allowed to use utensils, a cup, a plate, for example, or anything else that was used by a European. Even when any of the kitchen servants wanted to eat discarded leftover food; he had to use hands. For leftover coffee or tea, they were allowed to keep their own metal cups and teaspoons. Violating this prohibition was cause for dismissal from employment. Jim told Micah not to violate it, so in using the boss's toilet, he was taking a serious risk. Messing it up was even worse.

Micah was impressed with Peter's interest in learning new vocabulary words, which he got from reading his English Bible. He also noticed that Peter would sometimes ask Miss Moodie the meaning of some of the words, and she was more than happy to help him, although she seemed reluctant to spend too much time on that. Jim was a little older than Peter and less interested in reading. In fact he never bothered to read or learn new words. The other servants had no close contact with her.

On day soon after breakfast, she came into the kitchen to instruct Jim what to cook and prepare for lunch and supper. Micah summoned his courage and asked her a random question.

"Excuse me, Madam. How many teeth does an adult person have?" Micah asked. Miss Moodie looked at him and paused for a while, apparently searching for an answer in her mind. She smiled, raised a forefinger and said, "Wait, a minute." She opened the door to the dining room, walked out and closed the door behind her. After a few minutes, she returned, looked at Micah and said, "Thirty-two, sixteen, sixteen," while pointing at her upper and lower jaws. She smiled and resumed telling Jim what she wanted to eat for lunch and supper.

On her trip to a city of Umtali (now Mutare), she brought a book about a young Dutch boy, Micah's age, who was living on a farm, and a junior English dictionary. After breakfast, she came into the kitchen to give Jim the usual instructions on meals, called Micah and said, "Read this and ask me if you have any questions." Micah looked at her, suffered a mental block on what to say and simply clapped his cupped hands. That was customary and natural way for him to express deep gratitude. He had learned along the way that words sometimes cannot express the inner deep feelings. He had somehow learned what is meant by "Actions speak louder than words". She did not know what clapping of hands meant. She paused expecting Micah to say something. No word came out of Micah's mouth; he remained dumbfounded. Miss Moodie turned to Jim and started giving him instructions, after which she went out of the kitchen.

"Why didn't you say thank you? Are you stupid or something?" Jim asked, chiding him.

"But I clapped my hands; didn't I? That is what we always do; isn't it?" Micah defended himself.

On his spare time, Micah sat on the yard lawn under a tree, browsed the books, looked up into the sky and closed his eyes for a while. He could not believe what had happened. He had never had his own books before, certainly not a dictionary.

He looked for a piece of paper without success. He asked Peter for one, and he tore a piece from his notebook. Micah drafted a thank you note to Miss Moodie. *"Dear Madam: thank you much the book sorry I did not sat thank you I clapped hands.*" Micah said in his note. The next day he handed the note to Miss Moodie after she had finished talking to Jim. She just received the note and left the kitchen.

The book was written in very simple English and had large print and with colorful pictures and illustrations. It had a globe of the world and a map of north Western Europe and a brief description of the geography of Holland. Micah was fascinated to read about a small boy, eleven or twelve years old, living and helping his father feeding and milking the cows in summer and winter time and performing other duties on the farm. He stayed up late reading this book using candlelight and looking up some unfamiliar words. It was the first time that he had been exposed to geography of the world. Micah wished he was that boy or at least lived in the same environment. He jotted down question that came to mind as he read the book.

Within about two weeks, he had finished reading the book twice and had prepared a long list of questions to ask Miss Moodie. He kept that list in his pocket while working in the kitchen hoping for an appropriate opportunity to give it to Miss Moodie. For almost three or four days, she seemed in an awful hurry when she came into the kitchen for the usual talk with Jim. He dared not disturb her or seemed too much used to her for fear of being misunderstood by her, Jim or Peter.

Miss Moodie came into the kitchen the other day laughing and cracking jokes with Jim and Peter. Peter asked her the meanings of some words he had read in his Bible. She took a few minutes to define them for him. She was just about to leave the room when she turned around and, with her index finger pointing at Micah and asked, "Oh! Micah, did you like the book I gave you?" There was the opportunity he had been anxiously waiting for. "Yes," replied Micah handing her the list of questions he had been carrying in his pocket for several days. She received the list and disappeared behind the kitchen door.

After about a couple of hours, Micah was called into Miss Moodie's office portion of the lounge. She was sitting at her desk writing letters when she saw Micah coming through a large mirror on her desk, she turned around towards him. "Very good questions," she said looking at the list and seemingly intrigued by them. "What do you mean here?" she seemed puzzled by some of the questions. Apparently some of the questions were poorly phrased, and Micah tried to explain what he meant to say. It took her about an hour answering those questions she understood and ignored those that were not clear to her. The following week, she brought Micah a large hard-covered junior Encyclopedia and gave it to him during her round into the kitchen. He looked at her in disbelief and simply said, "Thank you much, Madam."

For several days, he stayed up late reading his encyclopedia. The room next door to his belonged to Wilson, Miss Moodie's driver. His girlfriend, Vaina, always visited him, especially on month-end, and stayed with him for several days. During all those nights Micah stayed up late reading, he overheard a moaning and groaning female voice that sounded like Vaina's. "Was she being physically abused or what?" Micah always wondered. Whatever was going on, the noise disturbed his studying. After several days of hearing the same sounds, Micah politely asked Wilson why he always beat up his girlfriend late at night. Wilson simply looked at Micah, and after a prolonged laughter said, "You are still too young to understand."

When Vaina visited Wilson again, she came with her sister three years younger than she was, but not younger than twenty years of age. While Micah was picking some green peas from the garden, Wilson approached him and said, "Micah, I have a problem. Vaina brought her sister with her, and I do not have a place for her to sleep. Please, help me out. Can she sleep on the floor in your room, just for one night?"

Micah thought about it for a few minutes and then said, "But I am embarrassed to share a bedroom with a woman. Besides my room is dirty, and I have a crude homemade bed with a mattress of dry grass. I cannot have a visitor in my room." Wilson assured him that she would not pay attention to such details in someone else's room. Micah then agreed to let her sleep in his room.

She knocked on Micah's door rather late at night, but since he was still reading, it did not seem to matter very much. He opened the door and let her in. He showed her a spot on the floor where she could spread a homemade mat and sleep. After a while he turned off the candle and fell asleep. In the middle of the night and in darkness, he woke up to someone's soft and warm hand fondling his private parts. A voice was repeatedly saying to his ears in a soft-spoiled whisper, "I cannot sleep. Wake up, please. Do it with me. Have you not done it before? I won't hurt you. Trust me. Let's do it, please."

For several weeks after that, everyone working for Miss Moodie talked about the incident and laughed at Micah saying, "Oh, he is not a man yet. He could not even do it. He was afraid of a woman. It seems he is not fertile and will never be able to impregnate a woman." Jim also joined in making fun of him, but Peter took him aside and praised him for resisting what he called "a temptation from the Devil". He went on to describe at length the Biblical story of Adam and Eve in the Garden of Eden.

Chapter 7

IT was not long before a timetable emerged. On many occasions Miss Moodie would ask Micah if he had questions from his readings. Micah tried to ask those questions he had verbally, but it became clear that it was better if he had them written down. So Micah did, and soon after breakfast during Miss Moodie's instructional period, he would hand them over to Miss Moodie. After a little while, she would open the kitchen door slightly and call Micah into her Study.

He had learned earlier that when you stand before your elders, you show them respect by your stance or the way you talk. Your manner of speaking would reveal your manners. A child was expected to avoid eye contact with an elderly person. Equally the same, an elder is supposed to avoid eye contact with a chief of the village. The practice of showing deference was the pillar for the cultural practice. A subordinate would even crawl on his knees, face down while clapping his hands to address a king or tribal chief. He would not dare look the chief in the face. The same practice was prevalent in the worshipping of God through the ancestral spirits.

Micah did not know how to stand in front of Miss Moodie. He was now alone in full view of his boss and with no object to shelter part of his body or to rest his arms or to lean against. So Micah decided to stand at attention, the military style, a distance away from her desk. He was very nervous to the point of being afraid for it was the first time for him to be exposed to a while person this close alone.

"These are very good questions, Micah," Miss Moodie broke the silence, which had prevailed for a while. Micah did not know what to say. He just mumbled something inaudible. "What?" Miss Moodie asked. Micah cleared his throat and said, "Thank you, Madam." She read the questions to herself aloud looking at Micah at the end of each question. The smile on her face reassured Micah that she was not threatening. However, he noticed that she had written something in red ink between his words. Miss Moodie started answering one question at a time. She spoke very slowly and enunciated all her words clearly with her eyes fixed on Micah's face. She took an hour to go through all those ten or so questions. "Do you understand?" she asked. There was a pause. "Now, go and read some more and bring more questions after two days," she said looking at her raised two fingers. She handed back to Micah a list of the questions.

"Thank you very much, Madam," Micah said with a smile and repeated one of the answers she had given to one of the questions to assure her that he had understood her explanations.

"You are very welcome. Now go back and continue washing the dishes," she said with an authoritative and serious voice. Micah turned around and walked away, and as he opened the door into the hallway leading to the kitchen, he looked back at Miss Moodie and noticed that she was also looking at him. She smiled broadly and Micah smiled back at her and closed the door behind him.

"Oh, where have you been all this time?" Jim asked with an air of sarcasm or a bit of jealousy. "The dishes and pots are still waiting for you. You did not expect me to help you wash them, did you? We all have our chores to do and if you do not finish yours on time, do not expect anyone to help you. Peter is busy in the bedrooms and will soon start on laundry. I am now preparing to cook lunch and I need to use some of those pots that are dirty and in the sink there," he went on and on talking. It was obvious he was not happy with what had happened and indeed on the pattern that was now developing between his junior on the job. After all, Micah was just a child. Why should he receive that much attention from Miss Moodie?

Three times a week, Miss Moodie would call Micah into her study for tutoring. She brought him English grammar books as well as books in arithmetic, science and social studies, and tutored him in all these subjects. She increased the tutoring time thus reducing number of hours he had to work in the kitchen or help Peter clean the house. That became a point of contention between Micah and other workers. Hard feelings became so obvious that Jim started making it hard for Micah to work there. He was Micah's direct supervisor and started nagging and criticizing him for insignificant things. He complained to Miss Moodie that Micah was now neglecting his duties in favor of studying.

"Micah, when you come for tutoring at 10 o'clock, bring all your books with you. You understand?" Miss Moodie said with a stern voice and without the usual smile. A chill went down Micah's spine. He looked at her. He looked at Jim and noticed a slight grin on his face. Peter picked up the tray, hurriedly opened the kitchen door and shut it behind him. The atmosphere was tense. Something was wrong somewhere.

"I must take these books away from you, Micah. You are spending too much time reading. You are neglecting your duties these days. What is wrong?" she asked. The air of seriousness on her face conveyed an unusual message. Micah knew that culturally he was not supposed to answer back to an elder, let alone your boss, or defend himself if that would be interpreted as arguing, being rude or disrespectful. He handed the books to her and stood there speechless.

"I am sorry, Madam," Micah said, his voice choking and with tears running down his cheeks. He did not know what else to say. There was a long pause, a very long pause.

"Do you want to go back to school?" she broke the long silence at last, and quickly added, "You do not have to answer that now." There was another pause. "Go back to the kitchen and work," she ordered. Micah walked away like a chicken that had been rained on.

"Have you ever read the Bible?" Peter asked. "Do you know some stories in this book?" Peter asked again raising his English Bible. "I will let you read it sometime when I am not reading it," he added without waiting for a reply from Micah. He described in detail the story of Joseph and his eleven jealous brothers as it is told in the Old Testament. Thus, Micah developed a keen interest in reading the Bible.

For several weeks, there was no direct communication between Micah and his employer. He had no books to read, except Peter's Bible. The Book of Psalms particularly attracted Micah's interest, for it seemed more relevant to what he was experiencing in his life. It seemed to speak and articulate his feelings for him.

One of Peter's responsibilities was to train Micah in how to perform all his duties so that whenever he was absent, Micah would take over and wait on Miss Moodie for meals, clean the bedrooms, bathrooms and the lounge as well as washing the dishes. Micah learned quickly how to perform these duties to the best of his capability and for his age level. Peter took two days off, and left Micah to assume his duties. Micah hated being left by himself to do all these tasks. For one thing, it was too much work and for another, it put him in the spotlight of things. He cleaned all the essential areas of the house and made Miss Moodie's bed as best as he could. He had just finished cleaning her bedroom for about an hour when she called him back. He knew right away that something had gone wrong by the way that Miss Moodie raised her voice.

Bending and pointing he finger under her bed, she ordered, "Take that, empty it in the toilet and clean it. Do that every time you clean my bedroom. Do you understand"? She walked out briskly and disappeared behind the door. Micah knew that he had not cleaned her chamber pot. He had not cleaned it the previous day on purpose which must have made her mad. Although Peter had instructed him to be sure that it was cleaned each day, Micah hated looking at an adult's urine. So he pretended that he had not noticed that it was there.

After about a month, Miss Moodie walked into the kitchen and said, "Micah, here is your English book. Do not neglect your duties while studying. You hear?" She handed him the book and walked out without looking at him in the face.

"Do you have some questions?" she asked another day.

"No, Madam," Micah replied while looking at Jim who seemed surprised by what she had said.

"Well, if you do, do not hesitate to ask me; all right?" she said with what seemed a forced smile and swung around to leave the kitchen. Before she completely disappeared behind the door, she stuck her head in the door and said, "You did not answer my question the other day. Do you want to go back to school next year?"

Micah managed to force a smile and replied, "Yes, Madam."

"Alright; I will talk to you about it some other time," she said and almost banged the door behind her.

Each day Miss Moodie came into the kitchen to give Jim her order for meals, she discarded some leftover food she no longer wanted or had spoiled. She placed what she didn't want on the table in the middle of the kitchen. It was Jim's decision as to what to do with the unspoiled leftover food. When he was in good mood, he would let Micah eat some of it. When he was not, he would either throw all of it in the sink or give all of it to the garden "boys". It later seemed like it was a way of getting at Micah for receiving some attention from Miss Moodie. Micah did not have some experience in telling when food was spoiled or not. Jim was an experienced cook and could tell either by looking at or smelling it. Whatever happened, Micah came down with a terrible stomachache. It usually would not have been a problem because his father and brothers had showed him certain roots or bulbs with medicinal properties. He looked for these around the plot, but could not find any. He did not want to tell anyone of this sickness, certainly not Jim for obvious reasons, although Micah knew that Jim had a lot of different types of medicine in his room.

In another compound there were three boys older than Micah. Because they came from the same area, a relationship had developed between Samson, one of the boys, and Micah. Somehow they had figured out that Samson was Micah's (sekuru) uncle. Micah would spend some of his off days with them, as he was not allowed to remain at Miss Moodie's compound when he was off. He confided in him, especially Samson, and a solid friendship had emerged between him and Micah.

It was natural therefore that Micah should go to Samson and tell him of his stomachache. Coincidentally, Samson had been suffering from stomachache for the previous week. He had been taken to the nearest clinic by Mrs. Edwards, his employer, and had been given some prescribed tablets. He had stopped taking the rest of them because he felt cured. Since it seemed like Micah had the same sickness, it was logical that he could also take the same medicine. Samson urged Micah to take two tablets at once because the sickness had just started. He did, and within a few minutes, Micah started vomiting seriously and continuously. The boys panicked and had to report the illness to Mrs. Edwards, but decided not to tell her about the tablets for fear of the consequences.

"What is your name, boy?" Mrs. Edwards asked. "Whom do you work for? What is wrong with you? How long have you been doing this? My God, he can't even talk! What did he eat? Do you know Samson?" she asked again and again. She suspected that Micah had been given some spoiled food by her "boys", if so then it could be worse. Samson and his friends did not dare tell her about the tablets. Micah would not dare tell on his uncle about it either. But that did not stop the vomiting, and seemed Micah was losing too much energy from throwing up.

"You boys know something. If you don't tell me now, this boy will die here and you will all go to jail. You hear; tell me! What did you give him?" she was furious. "Do you want me to call the police now?" she was now yelling at them. Meanwhile Micah was still vomiting outside on the lawn.

The "boys" looked at each other with fear, and Mrs. Edwards could now tell that they knew something. She inquisitively stared at each one of them for a minute or so, and when she stared at Samson he had to confess.

"His name is Micah. He works for Miss Moodie," he stopped talking and paused for a while.

"Come on Samson; go on. And—? What did you give him? He must not have been vomiting when he came here. Tell me now or I will go into the house and call the police," she threatened.

"I—I—a-give him some of those tablets I got from the clinic last week," Samson admitted.

"You gave him what? You told me you had finished taking all that medicine. Why did you do that, Samson? Are you a doctor or a nurse? What's the matter with you? If he dies here, you will also be executed; you know that?" she was now clearly angry with him. "I am going to call Miss Moodie right now, and you better know what you are going to tell her about this. This is very serious. Do you know that?" she stormed away into the house. She called Miss Moodie.

Within no time Miss Moodie's driver, Wilson, arrived to take Micah to the African clinic. As the car disappeared round the curve, Mrs. Edwards threw her last shot at Samson. "You better pray very hard that he does not die, or you are dead too," she shouted. There was no word from any of the boys.

It was determined that Micah was suffering from food poison which had been worsened by taking medicine prescribed to someone else. After questioning Micah and Jim, Miss Moodie found out that badly spoiled food caused the stomachache. Of course, she had never authorized any one to eat her leftover food.

It never became a laughing matter among the boys or anyone else in the neighborhood until after about two months when it was clear Micah had fully recovered. Jim was also now very cautious about the food he made available for people to eat. In fact, he did not want Miss Moodie to know that he gave away some leftover food. Peter warned Micah about trusting people that much. He and Jim had been nursing some sharp personality conflict pronounced by the religious differences and competition on the job. When Jim was away on his off days, Peter took the opportunity to explain to Micah complications of life in a way a brother would to his younger brother.

"Are you planning to go back to school at the end of the year?" Peter would ask. "You seem intelligent and would do well in school. Why did you drop out of school in the first place?" Peter wondered. "You know what? Miss Moodie said she is interested in you going back to school. Would you be interested in doing that?" he continued. He was just talking away while Micah was listening. Of course going back to school had been at the heart of Micah's plans. He just did not know how to go about it. Mr. Maikiri had aborted his plans the previous year. On the opposite side of the pendulum, the comfort and attention he was now experiencing at Miss Moodie's place seemed to threaten and sabotage his plans again. Would he return to school the following year? Was it not too late to make plans for doing that? Where would he get the money for fees and other expenses? Which school would take him having been out for a year and half now? Would he be able to find a home near a school, which would offer him accommodation? These are some of the questions that kept on lingering on his mind as he thought of school.

After a temporary break due to some misunderstandings, Miss Moodie resumed tutoring Micah in all three subjects, English, Arithmetic, and social studies. She soon declared it to everyone that ten o'clock in the morning was a tutorial time. That meant that Jim and Peter had to pick up the responsibility of washing dishes while Micah was attending the tutorials. This did not make them happy at all. It was now certain to everyone that Micah was going to return to school the following year.

"Do you know that I am preparing you for school?" she asked. "I got this syllabus from the headmaster of Melsetter African Primary School. It spells out the information you and children your age should know and skills you should have developed by now," she explained. Micah listened intently with his heart throbbing with happiness and excitement. He did not want to bring up the problem of money, but asked Miss Moodie to withhold most of his wages until the end of they year, just five months away. She agreed to do just that.

Chapter 8

DURING the colonial days, the government had two segregated ministries of education, one for the Europeans, and the other for Africans. The government was spending ten times more money on a European child over an African child. There were more European schools than there were African schools. The Europeans made up thirteen percent of the population. The Africans made up eighty-five percent; the remaining percentage was of the racially mixed people classified as Colored by the government. The three racial groups had separate everything, houses, hospitals, and schools. Only Europeans could vote; all Africans were disenfranchised. Basically all social services were free for the Europeans, and partially free for the Coloreds, but not so for the Africans. All fertile land belonged to the Europeans while Africans were pushed to live on dry, sandy, and rocky lands called African Reserves. Starvation, poor health and illiteracy were all commonplace in these areas. The natural resources of the country were being exploited and siphoned to the United Kingdom.

Thus the Africans started revolting against the colonial government and mobilizing themselves for independence. African nationalists formed political parties and were advocating for a one-man, one-vote franchise. But any African who opposed the status quo was arrested and locked up in detention camps or in prison often without court trial. Racial hatred was prevalent between the two groups. Those Africans who worked for the Europeans in the homes, in business or in mines were treated no better than slaves were. They worked for long hours for very little pay and no benefits. There were very few liberals like Miss Moodie. It therefore became a blessing to be employed by such Europeans.

"*Pamberi neChimurenga* (Forward with the Revolution)!" A nationalist leader, with a clinched fist waving in the air, would say when addressing a sea of people attending a mass political meeting.

"*Pamberi!* (Forward!)" The crowd would thunder in response also waving clinched fists in the air.

"*Pamberi vana vevhu!* (Forward the children of the *Soil!*)" The leader would shout. The term "child of the soil" was used to address an indigenous African who shared the same political views, rights and goals with others.

"*Pamberi!*" The crowd would answer back again in unison,

"*Pamberi nekubatana!* (Forward with unity!")

"*Pamberi!*"

The nationalist leader would address the people explaining colonialism and its effects on the lives of the Africans. He would try to inspire them into revolting against European rule and oppression.

Mass political rallies of that nature had become a common occurrence all over the country. Europeans hated that and engaged in vicious political propaganda against African activists. The government in turn let loose the police and informers everywhere to stifle and suppress African political activities. The lines were then drawn. Most other Africans deemed any favorable dealing with Europeans a sell-out activity. Therefore, there was to be no positive dealings between the oppressor and the oppressed, the colonizer and the colonized. There were to be no gray areas in between. Racial hatred was brewing, and it was obvious the seeds of civil and racial war were being sowed everywhere in the country.

Chapter 9

About three miles down the hill and across a relatively busy street lived a very prominent European farmer, Mr. Riebeck, known by the local Africans as Chapungu, the African name for an eagle. It was not clear why they called him that way. He was strict and feared not only by those Africans working for him, but also by any African who happened to be in his path.

Mr. Riebeck was very rich and had a large family of six children. Also on his farmhouse lived several members of his extended family. There were six vicious European type guard dogs either lying or roaming about in the yard. They were well fed and cared for, judging by their weight and health. They appeared friendly during daylight and to the Africans working on the farm household, but to strangers, they were fearsome. Mr. Riebeck supplied almost all other local Europeans with fresh vegetables, meat, and milk. Early in the mornings a string of African servants would be seen going in and out of the farm store with various supplies for their employers. The dogs were either trained to ignore all those people or were used to having these people come in and out of the farmyard.

One of the duties that Micah had to perform while working for Miss Moodie was going to collect one or two gallons of fresh milk every morning from Mr. Riebeck's farm. He hated performing this duty, not so much because he had to walk down the hill along a dusty and dirty path which resulted in his white tennis shoes being soiled each time he walked there. He hated going to this farmhouse for fear of the dogs there. He had no previous negative experience with dogs, but the thought of walking past these particular dogs lying there watching him sent a chill down his spine.

Hating it or not, Micah still had to perform that duty. He had been told over and over again that the dogs were friendly or did not bother anybody, if left alone. All one had to do was to mind one's business. For several months, he had managed to collect his courage and walk past those dogs with a jar of fresh milk. Of course, there was nothing to be afraid of, if you were innocent or just pretending to be while walking past them. This trick worked, of course, during daylight. At night it was a different ball game all together. There were stories of many African pedestrians or innocent passerby being bitten by Chapungu's dogs at night.

In fact, one African was killed having been attacked by these same dogs at night. Mr. Riebeck argued that the victim was a thief who was coming to steal from his yard or farm store. He was not prosecuted and his dogs were not punished either. Such was how cheap the African life was, so it seemed. The thought of all these stories lingered in Micah's mind each time he went to get some milk from there. He did not know what would trigger the dogs' anger or the urge to charge.

One Tuesday morning, Micah woke up early, got the fire started in the kitchen stove and under the water boiler, using wood and coal, and served Miss Moodie and her two visitors the early morning tea. Jim could now come into the kitchen and start preparing breakfast, and Peter could also start setting the dining table for breakfast. While these two were now doing their duties, Micah would then go and bring fresh milk from Mr. Riebeck's farm. When he brought the milk, Jim would use it to make coffee or boil it, ready for other needs that day. This was routine every day, and everything worked very well.

With some unusual level of energy, Micah partly walked and partly ran down the hill, crossed the road down below onto the plain on which Mr. Riebeck's house was built. He jumped over a small water furrow near the shade where Danai, one of the African servants, was giving out milk orders. He confidently walked past two or three dogs lying nearby and had his jug filled with some milk. He turned around and walked back the way he came. He kept his eyes on the dogs while walking very close to where they were lying down.

When he was just about to pass them, a big bulldog yawned and displayed his sharp teeth. The other one raised his head and growled. Micah panicked and started to run fast. He did not even hear Danai's loud voice telling him not to run. He looked back over his shoulder and saw a glimpse of one of the dogs running after him. He flew over the furrow but tripped over something and fell. He heard the dog barking and saw it coming. With reflex reaction, he rolled his body to lie on his back and just froze with fright. The dog stopped and stood stride over Micah until Danai and Mr. Riebeck's cousin ordered it to get off and stop growling. Micah finally got up unhurt but with a lot of embarrassment and heavily bruised pride. His shirt and khaki apron were all soaked wet with milk. He had lost control of his bladder and peed in his pants. His white pair of tennis shoes was all covered with dark-brown mud.

Mr. Riebeck telephoned Miss Moodie about the situation. She sent Peter for another supply of some milk and to walk Micah back to her house. The incident became a joke of the day around the compound for several months, but, to Micah, it was no laughing matter. He remembered it with embarrassment for a very long time. Miss Moodie subjected Micah to several lectures on bravery and how to respond to dogs, especially trained guard dogs. She bought booklets on different species of dogs, their temperament and likely reactions to human behaviors. It was an eye opener into the world of dogs, especially European breeds.

Chapter 10

The idea of returning to school never escaped Micah's mind, even when working for Miss Moodie seemed natural and satisfying. Under this employment, he had an assured shelter, a weekly supply of dry beans, upfu (fine cornmeal), ration beef (cheapest cut), salt and fresh vegetables from her garden. Those servants who worked in the kitchen (Jim, Peter, and Micah) were, in addition, supplied with a bar of laundry soap to ensure they had no excuse for wearing dirty uniforms. In addition, there was money to be earned at the end of each month, of course. With all these provisions being available and one's basic needs being met, it seemed foolish for one to leave that employment and be exposed to the harsh outside world.

As the year went by, the thought of going back to school became stronger and stronger on Micah's mind. But at the same time, the idea of leaving the security under Miss Moodie's employment was unthinkable as well. For a very long time, this dilemma weighed heavily on his mind.

During the month of November, Micah finally decided to return to school. But there were many problems and obstacles on the way. He dropped out of school in Sub B (Grade 2) and had now been out of school for two years. He had also grown older. Several questions started looming on his mind. Would he be able to catch up academically with other children of his age? Would his chronological age allow him to mix with other children in his grade level? Which school would he go to attend? The nearest, Mhakwe, was 15 miles away from the Muroti Area, where his parents lived, making it impossible for any child to walk to that school from there. He would have to find accommodation that was closer. Where would he stay? There were no relatives living near Mhakwe School. Would the money he had been saving last? What if the whole idea of attending school failed, and he again found himself in need of employment? Would his next employer be like Miss Moodie? The more he entertained these questions, the more he became confused and depressed.

"Excuse me, Madam. May I see you, please, after I finish my work," Micah said avoiding eye contact with his employer and almost resting his head on his left shoulder. Miss Moodie had just finished telling Jim what she wanted for lunch and supper and was about to walk out of the kitchen. With that unexpected request, everybody in the kitchen sort of froze. Jim and Peter glanced at each other with surprise. Jim displayed a sarcastic grin. There was a brief moment of silence.

"Yes. All right," Miss Moodie broke the silence. She seemed taken by surprise too. There was a long pause, an uneasy pause. She seemed to have detected an element of trouble and dejection in Micah. He did not look sick or anything. What was wrong? Could somebody have mistreated him or something? She looked at him with her militaristic nurse's eye. She could tell something serious must have been bothering him. She looked at Jim and then at Peter with an inquisitive eye, but she did not say anything. She turned around and looked at Micah again.

"E-e-eh, Micah, yes, you can see me when you come in for your lessons. Finish washing dishes. Go and get some fresh milk." Miss Moodie broke the uneasy silence and was clearly in charge of the situation. She patted Micah on the shoulder and quickly disappeared behind the kitchen door.

"*Iwe! Unodakutaurei naMadamu?* (You! What do you want to say to Madam?)," asked Jim, with an air of scolding mixed with an element of jealousy and sarcasm. Micah did not reply to the question. He looked at Peter and mumbled something inaudible. Peter just looked at Jim and then at Micah. He then shrugged his shoulders, as if to say to Micah, "I have nothing to do with that question."

For sometime it had appeared that other servants on the compound were starting to dislike Micah either out of jealousy or suspicion. They resented the fact that he was getting too much attention from a European over them. Indeed, the relationship between him and Miss Moodie had developed from that of employee-servant to that of student-mentor. The feeling his colleagues now had seemed to have some political and social connotations to it. He could be an informer on the political and employment levels, they thought. Was he still one of them (Africans, servants)? Had he become somehow special and, if so, why? In the whole compound and the small town of Melsetter, Micah had begun to feel isolated by his African colleagues and friends.

"*Ko, chii chirikukunetsa mazuva ano? Zvaitasei*, Mika? (What is troubling you these days? What is wrong, Micah?)" Peter asked, while the two were walking together to the compound, the other day. They suddenly stopped and turned to face each other. Micah avoided eye contact with Peter. He hesitated to reply for he was not sure how Peter would respond to how he felt inside.

"*Ndirikuda kudzoka kuchikoro. Zvino handizivi kuti ndoitasei* (I want to go back to school. Now, I do not know what to do," Micah replied with his head tilting to the side. "*Uye, vanhu vavakundivenga. Handizivi kuti ndatadza chii* (Also, people seem to hate me now. I do not know what I have done wrong)," he added with tears beginning to gather in his eyes.

To console him, Peter told the story; he had read in the Bible, about Joseph and his twelve brothers. Joseph's father had bought him a coat of many colors. His brothers started hating him for that, and conspired to kill him. Because of the older brother's pleading, they finally agreed to sell him to Egypt instead. Micah listened intently to the story. Peter offered to let him borrow his Bible and read for himself about Jesus and other stories.

"What did you want to see me about?" Miss Moodie asked before she started answering Micah's questions on the Geography of Holland and the shape of the world.

"I want to go back to school next year, Madam," Micah said politely without looking her in the eye. He had learned a long time ago that it was a sing of disrespect to have a direct eye contact with an adult or boss. And so it had become a habit to avoid eye contact with older people. Miss Moodie's face just beamed with a broad smile and looked at him for a while before saying anything. Micah did not know what that meant. But the smile assured him that she was happy to hear that. Her response was sweet music in Micah's ears.

"Good boy, Micah!" she said with some excitement. "When do you want to go back to school? Which school will you attend? Which grade will you be in? That is very good, Micah. I have been wondering myself about whether or not you were interested in going back to school. You are such a bright boy. You would do well in school. What do you want to be when you get your education? Do you have an idea yet?" she fired a lot of questions Micah could not answer. He was sure of one thing, going back to school the following year.

"I want to go back to school in January when the school term starts. The nearest school from my home is Mkakwe. I will look for accommodation close to it. "Can I stop working here in time to start school?" Micah asked. He could not answer all the other questions she had asked. Miss Moodie said there would be no problem. She would be glad to let him go at the end of December.

Micah felt highly relieved to know that Miss Moodie was glad to know his wishes and plans, and that she would let him go. The lessons that day went very well. For the first time in many months, Micah's future seemed bright. He felt like a heavy load had been lifted off of his shoulders. He was highly elated and excited about the turn of events. He now had something to look forward to.

When he walked out of the lounge, his face was shining with happiness and confidence. Peter and Jim saw him dashing out through the kitchen hoping and jumping all the way to his room in the compound. Other servants who saw him could tell that something had happened to Micah. He had never been this way before. He ran straight to his room, threw himself on his crude homemade bed and rejoiced. Suddenly it dawned on him that there were still some problems and hurdles to be overcome. He remembered the previous experience with Mr. Maikiri, almost a year ago. Then some of the rays of light seemed to disappear from the horizon. Nonetheless, he still had reasons to be happy. The road back to school had been cleared. Miss Moodie had been saving part of his wages, and this should enable him to attend school. Thus, from there on he started preparing for school.

Chapter 11

There was not much preparation to speak of. School calendar started in mid-January and ended in December before Christmas. A pupil would need uniform, stationery and money for tuition fees in order to attend school. Micah felt he had enough money to take care of all these, at least for one year. He felt confident about the situation, and for the rest of the period he worked for Miss Moodie, he felt great. Everything that was going on at the compound did not affect his morale. He was set to go back to school.

"Micah, you need to go and visit your parents before you start school in January. When was the last time you saw your parents? I am sure you must have been missing them all this time; don't you?" Miss Moodie asked a series of questions without waiting for answers.

He looked at the floor, seemingly avoiding eye contact with her. There was nothing unusual about that. Micah had always been doing that all the time. But what was unusual about this is the long silence that occurred. When he lifted his head, there was an air of sadness on his face. A close look at his eyes would have revealed a trace of tears in his eyes. Why was he sad? Why was he almost to the point of tears at the mention of the idea of visiting his parents? A child of his age would have missed his/her parents. In fact, he would not have left home in the first place to be employed far away. Thus Miss Moodie expected him to jump with excitement at the mention of his parents.

"You will stop working for me at the end of December. Go and see your mother and father," she said, almost ordering him. "I will give you your money when you return from home, and then you go to school," she added.

It seemed like she was talking to her own child. She waited for a response. There was silence. She turned her face away and coughed several times, reached for a facial tissue, and cleaned her mouth and nose. When she suddenly turned around to face him, she caught him looking at her. She asked him why he seemed unhappy.

"I do not want to go home," Micah finally replied. "I am afraid my father will keep me at home or stop me from going back to school," he added, almost crying. Miss Moodie did not say a word. She just asked him to return to the kitchen and continue with his usual duties.

It was very emotional for people on the compound to see Micah leave, and so it seemed. Micah wiped a tear or two. Miss Moodie just stoically stood at the kitchen door and said "Goodbye". An old crowded bus turned around the corner on a heavily dusty road to the bus stop. After off loading all the passengers, it loaded again ready to return to Umtali (now Mutare), about sixty miles away via Chief Muusha's area where Biriwiri Mission Station was located. The bus was covered with a lot of dust, both inside and outside, since it traveled on dusty roads all the time. There were two goats and several chickens loaded on top of the bus. Micah looked at the seat where he was to sit. He looked at his clean khaki short trousers. He almost would not have sat down had it not been for other passengers who were pushing him from behind as they sought for an unoccupied seat. He was worried about cleanliness, as laundry could be a problem later. He was not sure about the situation ahead of him. There was no choice but to find a seat quickly before the bus started off. He did very reluctantly. The bus took almost one hour to travel twenty miles over a range of mountain characteristics of the Eastern Highlands of the country. The ride was extremely bumpy and uncomfortable, but comfort was a luxury many passengers did not dream of. Just to be able to afford the fare and find a seat on the bus was enough. Many passengers traveled while standing all the way to the door risking injury in case of an accident. Frequent stops contributed to the slowness of the bus.

Micah got off the bus and had to walk seven miles of dusty road to Mhakwe School. There was no bus service along that road, so people walked or used bicycles, scotch carts and wheelbarrows for transportation. That was not new or unusual to him. He had experienced all these in his life. The only difference is that for a year he had lived under the shelter of a European in an urban setting. He had read about how other people in other continents, especially Europe, lived. He had read about a small boy who lived on a farm in Holland. He had had a glimpse of life far easier to live than what he was now seeing again.

Mr. Moyo was the headmaster of a Baptist Church Mhakwe School. He was a short and baldheaded middle aged man who walked with an air of authority and pride. He was in his office, apparently getting ready for the beginning of the school term. His visitor hesitated to approach and knock on the door, which was partially open. The windows were all wide open to allow a cool late afternoon breeze in his office. The visitor finally collected his courage; in fact, he had no choice. This was it, what he had been waiting for, and the school. This was the man who was in charge, and this was his office.

Micah extended his arm and knocked on the door. "Who is it? Come in," a rather intimidating voice boomed from behind the desk. He stepped inside, still carrying his suitcase and bag on each hand. "Who are you? Can I help you?" Mr. Moyo said studying the seemingly intruder from top to bottom. There was a brief pause, and Mr. Moyo impatiently repeated, "Can I help you? What is your name? Where are you from? Put your bag and suitcase on the floor."

His visitor did not know what to do with his now free hands. It was grossly impolite to put one's hands in the pockets in front of an elder or a person in authority. He did not know which stance or pose would be in favor with this headmaster. Within a few seconds of uneasiness, he tried almost every pose and arms position he could think of, all in the eyes of the educator. Mr. Moyo must have discerned a sign of nervousness in his visitor for there was a seemingly forced grin on his face.

"I am Micah Chinoda from Muroti, e-e-eh, from Melsetter. I am looking for admission into your school, Sir," he managed to speak. He avoided eye contact with Mr. Moyo, and his head was tilted to his left shoulder.

"Which grade? How old are you? Do you have a birth certificate? Do you have a transfer letter? Where will you live while attending this school? Do you have money for school expenses?" One question came after another.

Micah felt a chill down his spine. Just as he feared, he did not have good answers to any of those questions. He had dropped out of school before completing Standard two, and he had spent two years out of school. He did not know how old he was for his parents were illiterate and there was no birth certificate on record anywhere. He was sure of one thing, he had grown older. A transfer letter could be obtained, but that would create a problem for it would place him back in standard two. He did not want that. The idea was for him to skip Standard two in order to match the Standard level with his chronological age. As to the question of accommodation, he told him that he had some relatives near the school who would provide him with accommodation. He had the money for school and hoped that it would be enough. If not, he would work during the school holidays in the area there.

Micah admitted to the headmaster that he did not know his date of birth, but would check with his relatives. He told him that a transfer letter would be difficult to get and was likely to delay his entrance back into school. To compromise, Mr. Moyo said the applicant would therefore have to take Standard three tests for entrance into Standard four. Micah would have to come back the following morning to take the test.

The truth of the matter was Micah did not have anywhere to go for the night. He would need some time to look for accommodation before the school started in two weeks time. It was too late in the day to arrange it for the night. So he had to bite the bullet. He told the headmaster where he had just come from and then asked him for a place to spend the night. Mrs. Moyo was a very hospitable lady. In fact, she labored at length to try and trace some kind of kinship with the visitor. Despite the hospitality, Micah could not sleep well. His mind was on the pending entrance test. He rehearsed in his head as much of the lesson he had had with Miss Moodie throughout the year. Although she did not have a curriculum grade, she covered a lot of English grammar, some Arithmetic and Social Studies at a level that was appropriate for Micah.

Miss Moodie had to have been prophetic because the test, which Micah was about to take, was mainly on Arithmetic and English, with a sprinkle of Social Studies and Current Affairs here and there. He had really never taken a formal test. For a moment he almost froze out of nervousness. Then he started sweating terribly despite Mr. Moyo's urging to stay calm and his assurance that everything would be all right. He graded the test while Micah was seated in the shade of a nearby Musasa tree waiting. It seemed like he took forever to grade it. He called Micah back into his office, offered him a seat and stared at him without saying a word. Micah's heart was pounding with fear for the worst.

Then suddenly, the headmaster broke into a broad smile and said, "U-u-ugh, what a student. You did very well. I did not expect this, given the background you told me yesterday. Here are your test papers. There is no problem. You can go into Standard Four." Micah smiled and could almost jump for joy but was afraid of the impression it would create in the headmaster's mind. He knew that he owed this success to Miss Moodie, and he felt indebted to her forever.

The headmaster went on to explain to Micah the tuition fees, the uniform and stationery that were required. In addition to all these, however, there was a building fee. The parents of the area had agreed to raise funds to build a classroom block for Standards four to six. Every household had to pay that fee at the beginning of the year. The amount he mentioned hit Micah on the head like a ball of lead. It was far beyond what he could afford. He did not know about all this and therefore had not saved that kind of money while working for Miss Moodie. How on earth could he come up with that much money?

A brief moment of elation from passing the test was suddenly transformed into despair. Mr. Moyo noticed the level of dejection in him and slowly walked around his desk back to his chair. He sat down and pretended to be busy by fumbling some papers on his desk. With tearing eyes, Micah managed a faint smile. He looked at Mr. Moyo and said, "Thank you very much, Sir." He grabbed his bag and suitcase and walked out.

Chapter 12

The elders in Micah's rural village had a saying, "*Natsa kwawabva kwaunoenda husiku* (Leave the previous place in good order because where you are going is nightfall. You do not know what lies ahead)." In the old days, people walked for miles from village to village. Every home was expected to extend some hospitality to travelers, strangers, or otherwise. Travelers would be given food, a place to sleep and a send-off provision for the journey the next day. The travelers would reciprocate the hospitality by being polite and respectful and by extending a traditionally acceptable good-bye when leaving. That way should anything go wrong on the way to the next village, the travelers could return to where they had spent the night before and be welcomed again. Burning bridges where one had been guaranteed doom ahead.

When Micah left Miss Moodie's place, he made sure that he did not step on anyone's toes. It was an emotional departure, and it appeared in conformity with the African traditional custom and requirement. Could he come back and be welcomed by his colleagues or were they glad he had left? Could Miss Moodie offer him employment again?

The fact that Micah did not have money for building fee meant that the prospect for resuming school had slipped away from him. If that happened, would he ever have any chance of pursuing his education? As he mechanically walked away from Mr. Moyo's office, he was confused and dejected. He did not know where to go or what to do. It seemed like the heavens had fallen; there was total darkness ahead of him. As if by instinct, Micah walked towards the dusty road that led back to where he got off the bus the previous day.

Peter and Jim were somehow shocked to see Micah back at Miss Moodie's house. They managed to say almost at the same time, "*Ko, *wadzokasei*? (Why have you come back?)" He only said, "*Handina mari yakakwana yechikoro.* (I do not have enough money for school.)" At this point he started crying openly. The dialogue attracted the attention of Miss Moodie who visibly displayed sadness and surprise. She immediately beckoned for him to come inside the house and into her lounge where she used to tutor him.

"What is the matter? Why have you come back? You could not find a place in school? What happened?" she kept firing lots of questions before Micah could answer any one of them. He collected himself, wiped off tears from his eyes and explained to her the whole problem. He gave her the graded entrance test papers. She examined them very carefully, broke into a broad smile and patted him on the shoulder. "Well done, Micah. I am proud of you," she said with her right hand touching his left shoulder.

"May I have my job back, please, Madam," Micah interrupted. "I cannot afford school. I don't even know when I was born. I want to work, instead. Please, please Madam, take me back," he pleaded almost in tears again.

She ignored everything he was saying. She reached for her desk and got out a pen and writing pad. She started writing what appeared to be a letter. Then she picked up her purse from the floor and got out some money. She enclosed some of the money and the letter in an envelope. She wrote the words "The Headmaster" on the back of the envelope. She got up from the chair and faced him and said, "Here is the money you need. Go back to Mhakwe School and give this letter to the headmaster there. Come and work here during the school holidays." With that, she lightly pushed him away towards the door and walked him out of the house. He did not have time to talk to his former colleagues for he had to hurry to catch the bus. He ran as fast as he could to the bus station and managed to board the bus, as it was just about to pull out of the rank.

Mr. Moyo was busy with some parents in his office. Micah waited outside firmly holding an envelope in his hand, as if he feared someone would snatch it away from him. The headmaster ushered his visitors outside as they were leaving his office. He caught sight of Micah standing rather obscurely around the corner of the building. "Oh! You are back. Come in. I thought you had gone away for good," he expressed his surprise. He stretched his hand to receive the envelope from Micah. He hurriedly opened it. His face suddenly turned into a broad smile. With some money in one hand, he scrutinized the contents of the letter. Then he exclaimed, "Congratulations, young man! You are blessed. You must thank God. This European lady says she will pay for your school expenses, if you make good grades. God has blessed and opened the door for you," he repeated while looking at Micah in the eye. "Oh, you are twelve years old; right? I will mail the receipts to Miss Moodie. School starts on Wednesday next week. I will see you then," Mr. Moyo dismissed him with a hand gesture.

Micah did not know what to say in response to Mr. Moyo. He just quietly walked out of the door. He was just too dumbfounded to say anything. He absentmindedly walked to a nearby tree and sat down in the shade to allow the turn of events to sink into his mind. He could not believe what the headmaster had just told him. How did Miss Moodie come up with his age? He wondered. As he carefully thought about it, he remembered her telling her brother, Brigadier George, approximately how old she thought Micah was when he started working for her. His junior certificate had not helped her find out his age. So she had to estimate his age.

Chapter 13

In the traditional African culture, kinship could be two pronged. It could be established on either bloodline (direct genetically descended) or on *totem* line. The traditional African family was made up of extended kinship. It would have parents, children, uncles, aunts, and nephews, nieces, and cousins all regarding each other as being closely relationship. The word cousin did not exist in their vocabulary because it distanced relatives. The kinship circumference ended at the nephew/niece level. On your father's side were *Baba* and the *babamukuru(s)* and *babamunini(s)* (father, older fathers, and younger fathers, respectively). On your mother's side were the uncles, nephews, and nieces. Since in this culture, the family was patriarchal, the father's side of the family was more important. That is why a male child was preferred to a female one. The male would perpetuate a close knit family, thereby enlarging one's generation.

The concept of totem involved a close relationship between humans and animals or other living creatures. After all they shared this world that was given to them by *Musikavanhu* (the Creator of the people). Thus some people would adopt a certain animal such as a lion, porcupine, cow, monkey and they would be addressed by that totem (Shumba, Ngara/Maposa, Sithole, or Soko, respectively). Others would adopt birds as their totem in the same way. Those who shared the same totem would regard each other as being related even though they were not blood relatives. Thus, with intensive genealogical research, one could practically establish some form of kinship with almost anybody in the region or country. Establishing relationship this way made it easier for a traveler or stranger to find social support anywhere in the country.

Mr. Mawosa had a family of four children, small by the traditional African standard. His homestead was located near Mhakwe River and a dusty road that linked the school with Melsetter and Umtali. He had been exposed to the Baptist Church for quite a while. In fact, he was regarded as one of the elders of the local Church at Mhakwe School which was just four miles away from his home. He was an Agricultural Demonstrator by profession whose duties included showing the local peasant farmers modern farming methods and organizing meetings. At such meetings, a government official in the Ministry of Lands would meet with local Africans and pass on to them colonial Government requirements and expectations. Some people hated him for they regarded him as an arm of what they saw as an oppressive Government. Other, of course, respected him and appreciated his efforts to help them become better producers of foodstuffs.

During the conversation with Mrs. Moyo on the day Micah spent the night at her house, Mr. Mawosa's name came up as a possible provider for accommodation. As he sat under that tree, upon leaving Mr. Moyo's office, he recalled that name. Yes, he needed somewhere to stay while going to school. Why not try Mr. Mawosa for an accommodation? After all he was a churchman and was likely to be kind and willing to help. The last thought gave him wings to fly to his home.

Mr. Mawosa had one of the best and fertile fields in the area, and since he was a man of agriculture, he had become famous for heavy harvests. Many people from far and near came to work in his field for money, maize, wheat, and *mhunga* (indigenous grain) or other foodstuffs. He needed a lot of people to provide that labor force, and Micah would be one of them.

"*Ndinotsvagawo pekugara ndichiinda kuchikoro* (I am looking for a place to stay while attending school)," Micah requested when asked what he wanted. Mr. Mawosa did not seem hesitant to offer him where to stay, but quickly went on to lay down the conditions under which he would be accommodated. Micah accepted the conditions, and was determined to abide by them so that he could stay in school. Nothing would be in his way this time.

The first day of school was great and full of excitement. Mr. Moyo called the names of students going into the newly created two streams of Standard Four. He assigned them to either Four A or Four B stream, depending on their performance during the previous year. Four A stream was for those who were considered academically gifted or had performed above the average. Micah was assigned to Four A, and was exhilarated to an extent of almost jumping for joy. It was an honor to be classified among those students who had never had to drop out of school. The headmaster's assistant gave him two sets of the uniform, all necessary books and stationery. To his surprise, very few students were issued with all books and stationery because they did not have enough money to pay for them. Some could not afford even one set of the uniform.

His teacher, Mr. Munhutu, seemed very nice. He obviously carried an air of authority and of a disciplinarian. Four A class was better furnished than Four B; in fact, a lot better than all other classes in the school. It had enough benches for 35 pupils. Other classrooms had very few benches and no desks. In such cases, some pupils had to sit on the floor and read or write while resting their books and papers in their laps. Micah did not take long before he fully adjusted to the school routine and requirements. He quickly made some friends as well.

Because the country was a British colony, all schools were formal and militaristic, a replica of the British discipline. Pupils were expected to be extremely polite to the school authorities, including teachers and visitors. They had to stand at attention when the teacher, headmaster of visitor walked into the classroom and, in unison said, "Good morning/afternoon Sir/Madam!" The authority would respond, "Good morning/afternoon, children. Be seated." The pupils would reply in unison, "Thank you, Sir/Madam," and sit down. They had to stand up to answer or ask a question, or just to make a point during class discussion.

Corporal punishment and manual work after school was the order of the day, especially for breaking the school rules or acting up in class. Failure to do one's homework or to memorize assigned work was punishable by a paddle on the buttocks, palms or fingertips. Sekai, one of the girls in Standard 4B, failed to perform some mental Arithmetic problems using a time's table. Her teacher, Mr. Mukwambo, paddled her so severely that she went home with her palms full of red blisters.

When the bell rang for break or recess, the pupils sighed with relief and rushed to the playground. There they chased each other, wrestled one another to the dusty ground. Boys took advantage of that to flirt with girls and pinched their bottoms. Some girls cried and ran back into the classrooms.

Before leaving Mr. Mawosa's home for school each day, Micah was expected to perform some work in the field or vegetable garden, tend the cattle and sometimes help out in the kitchen, since Mrs. Mawosa did not have any helpers. That meant waking up very early in the morning. After school, he would then do the bulk of his duties until dusk. Since the school started at eight in the morning and ended at one o'clock in the afternoon, it meant putting in a lot of hours each day, all to pay for accommodation and food only. On Saturday, he would work from dawn to dusk, just like other workers there. Sunday was a relatively off day, except that the cows still had to be milked and driven to and from grazing areas. His two sons, one older and the other one younger than Micah, did not have to spend that much time doing chores. They were in their own home, anyway.

With all the work Micah had to do and the time he had to spend on it, he increasingly found it difficult to study, let alone to do homework. He simply had very little time and energy left to do homework or study. In class he could not concentrate and therefore his performance level began to decline. He had to decide on how to balance between working for food and accommodation and maintaining good grades in school. Which master was he to be more loyal to, Mr. Mawosa's work or schoolwork? How could he serve both equally? What would be the consequences of the actions he took to remedy the situation? He decided to go slow on Mr. Mawosa's work so that he could reserve energy and time for schoolwork. He lacked the tactic needed in striking the balance between effort and time.

Before six months time was over, Micah had to leave and look for another home that would perhaps allow him time for schoolwork. Little did he realize that finding such a home would be extremely fastidious because it would depend on recommendation from Mr. Mawosa. Besides, most families would only welcome a person who provided them with maximum manual labor, not a dependent or someone in need of humanitarian treatment. Was there a possibility that some family somewhere near the school was related to him somehow? Micah wondered.

In an area called Matanho, about five or six miles away from school, there lived Mr. Nhongo. His wife had died leaving him with two sons, Johane and Robson. He had then married a partially deaf lady, many years his junior. Two beautiful young girls had been born of this second marriage. They were both very active churchgoers, and Mr. Nhongo was on the parents' school committee together with Mr. Mawosa.

Someone at the school tipped Micah that Mrs. Nhongo's totem was Ngara/Maposa (porcupine). That would mean that she shared the same totem/porcupine with him, and therefore the two were related. Should he beg for accommodation from this family? He wondered. He decided to try his luck even though he feared that there might be an adverse recommendation from Mr. Mawosa.

He approached the couple, and first introduced himself as the son of Nyemudzai, a Maposa, who lived in Muroti area. Mrs. Nhongo said she had heard of him as being one of the Maposa people living in that area, but had not met him. Sure enough there was some kinship there, although distant. They wholeheartedly welcomed him into their home, and added that he could stay there for as long as was necessary. Even though Micah told them that he had been staying with Mawosa's family, they did not seem interested in a recommendation from him. They did ask him, however why he had left in the middle of the year. After he had been staying with them for two weeks, Mrs. Nhongo confided in Micah that Mr. Mawosa had vigorously opposed their offering him accommodation on the ground that he was lazy and dishonest on the job. She urged him not to worry about that for it was known in the area that Mr. Mawosa exploited his workers.

The Nhongo's grew enough crops to feed their family. They had cattle, goats, and some chickens and fairly fertile field. Their expectations of the school-going-age children were completely the opposite of those in Mr. Mawosa's home. They would assist adults working in the fields and in the vegetable garden. For full-fledged household work and domestic animal tending, Mr. Nhongo relied on hired service. That was solace to Micah who had been craving for more time to do schoolwork. His grades soared, and his teacher told Mr. Moyo the dramatic change he noticed in his work. The headmaster called him to his office and told him that he was writing a letter to Miss

Moodie, and that if he wanted to he could do the same. He did and handed the letter to the headmaster the following day.

The one-roomed house that Johane and Robson slept in had one homemade bed and mattress. It had mud covered floor, which needed to be attended to periodically. Usually, most women would mix cow dung in water and use the thickened mixture to smear such floors. When the mixture dried, it hardened and the floor assumed the texture and appearance of one smeared with cement. However, this condition would not be durable, hence the need to periodically work on it the same way. Somehow, such manual work overwhelmed Mrs. Nhongo, and she did not get around to doing the house floors as often as was needed.

To make the situation worse, Johane and Robson, and occasionally Micah too, would dance to their favorite music on that floor, thereby tearing it up fast and further damaging it. Before long, the floor just became dilapidated and unhygienic. Pretty soon maggots, fleas, and other tropical insects started growing and living in that broken-down floor. Blankets and other covers collected a lot of dust and also became a habitat to these parasites. The boys, especially Micah who slept on the floor, became prey to all these. It is amazing how the human body can develop insensitivity and immunity to all these. The boys would develop big pimples on their skins, and occasionally would catch some of those parasites. They would be red and pregnant with blood.

Despite these unfavorable bedroom conditions, the atmosphere at this home was conductive to education. Micah was treated like he was one of the Nhongo's children. He offered a lot of help to Johane who was in Standard 4B class. Once in a while, Johane covertly expressed an element of jealousy in the fact that Micah was in the stream class and performed consistently better than he did. It was just a boys or children's thing, and nothing to worry about.

During the course of the year 1960, political activities intensified throughout the country. African political parties were formed and banned by the government. Several African political leaders were either thrown into detention camps or imprisoned without trial. Nevertheless, defiance was the order of the day. Africans in urban and rural areas were mobilized and sometimes coerced to attend mass political rallies.

Children were also expected to attend such meetings since they were to be future participants and political leaders of the country.

On Thursday, before pupils left school, the headmaster announced that political leaders from Salisbury (now Harare) and Umtali (Mutare) were organizing a mass political rally to be held near the school the following day. Every pupil at Mhakwe School and adults in the area were expected to attend. The whole school was dismissed shortly before break time, and pupils and teachers were ordered to the rally. All paths led to the spot where the rally was to be held. Seemingly endless streams of people flowed from all directions. Before long, there was a sea of men sitting on rocks or logs and women sitting on the ground facing a crudely constructed artificial platform. For two hours people patiently waited while singing revolutionary songs, but no visiting leaders were in sight. They began to be disenchanted and felt cheated. When five leaders finally arrived in an entourage, some people were already starting to disperse.

"*Pamberi neChimurenga*! (Forward with the Revolution!)" The highest ranking local political leader signaled the start of the rally.

"*Pamberi*!" the people thundered back in unison with fists in the air.

"*Pamberi VanaVevhu*! (Forward the Children of the Soil!)"

"*Pamberi*!" they responded.

Then someone from the crowd started to sing an inspirational revolutionary song, and everyone responded. The atmosphere in the area was filled with waves and waves of voices from the crowd. This went on for twenty or thirty minutes. The visiting speakers were then introduced in the order they were to address the audience.

"*Pamberi nekubatana*! (Forward with unity!)"

"*Pameri nemwana wevhu* (Forward with a child of the Soil), the first speaker bellowed.

"*Pamberi*!" the crowd answered while creating waves in the air with their arms.

The speaker enunciated what he called the evils of colonialism, and the oppression inflicted on the Africans. He reminded his listeners that they were totally disenfranchised and were innocent sheep on their own land, and the Europeans were hungry wolves in the process of devouring their prey. The Europeans were exploiters of the natural resources of the country, vapambi vevhu (the snatchers of the Soil). They were parasites.

Just as he was about to complete his speech, and to the people's surprise, two government vehicles, each with five policemen and four vicious dogs, arrived. The policemen armed with riot batons and dogs, agilely jumped out of their jeeps and headed straight for the platform. The one who seemed to be the leader announced that the rally was illegal and subversive, and therefore was prohibited by law. He added that the organizers were under arrest. With an authoritative gesture, he ordered the dog-handlers to use the dogs to disperse the crowd forthwith. The crowd broke into pandemonium and panicked. The pupils were frightened and started running in all directions. The adults were horrified to see how the police, eight of whom were Black, mishandled and humiliated their leaders as they led them away to the vehicles.

Chapter 14

Mr. Mwakutuya, a well-known building contractor in the Mhakwe area, started erecting a six-classroom block on what used to be a soccer field. Pupils would gather around during break to watch his builders working. Within three months, the building was completed, to the exultation of the parents and students as well. This building project was what the building fee was for and had almost denied Micah an opportunity to resume schooling.

Mhakwe School was a feeder school for Rusitu Mission, ninety miles away. After Standard Three, pupils (students) would go to a boarding school at Rusitu Mission for Standards Four, Five and Six. With the new building completed, the school would now be upgraded, and would keep its students for three years. The plan was foiled at the end of the school year when only fifty percent of the students in the two streams in Standard Four passed. The school could not create a Standard five class in this case. Before school closed for the December holiday, the school board had to make a decision on what to do with those who had passed Standard Four.

Word soon went around that the board had ruled that Mhakwe School would have four classes of Standard Four, two consisting of repeaters and the other two made up of those students moving up from Standard Three. The question was where would those who had passed Standard Four go for Standard Five? That was the question which lingered on the minds of the parents and students who were affected.

Micah was one of those who did not know where they would go for Standard five the following year. With that uncertainty, nevertheless, Micah went to Melsetter for the December school holiday. The atmosphere at Miss Moodie's home was now different from what it was the previous year. She had not replaced him on the job, and that did not please Jim and Peter who were used to having an assistant in the kitchen. When he arrived back from school, Jim was somehow lukewarm in his attitude towards him. Peter reacted just about the same towards him, as an advisor and religious model. Micah was surprised to hear that he now had a nickname, Moodie's Boy, and that everyone in that small town had started calling him by that name. Perhaps some people had given him that nickname out of jealousy and envy, and perhaps others had done so in acknowledgement of Miss Moodie's role in his life. Whatever the reasons, Micah did not seem to mind. Being called Moodie's boy or Moodie's child was fine with him; in fact, he loved it.

Judging from the way Miss Moodie treated him, the nickname seemed appropriate. She just embraced him at least as his guardian and did not hide that fact. His duties had now changed to cater for his need for time to study, and attend further tutorial sessions with her. She instructed Jim to let Micah eat some leftover food, only when it was necessary. He still had to fend for himself as far as other needs were concerned. Obviously, Miss Moodie did not want to spoil the young African child.

A few days before Christmas, a letter came from the Mhakwe School headmaster stating that Micah had been assigned to go to Rusitu Mission boarding school for standard five. What a Christmas gift it was. Fortunes seemed to have descended on Micah like manna from Heaven. He was just baffled over the turn of events during the last two years. Micah wondered what it was that had made things turn out to be that way.

As Peter was going down to his compound, usually to pray, Micah followed him. He told Peter how he had managed to pass the entrance test into standard four skipping standards two and three. He revealed that Miss Moodie had pledged to pay all his school expenses and that she had started doing so with Mhakwe School. He related how the accommodation problem worked out at Mhakwe. He told him how well he passed standard four and that now he had been assigned to attend Rusitu Mission boarding school.

"Micah, you are being blessed! God is being good to you, Micah! Do you see that? He is doing all these things for you. You must pray and thank Him for all that," Peter seemed spiritually possessed as he went on and on trying to help Micah see the hand of God in what was going on. "Let us pray, Micah, let us pray," he said with a lot of excitement and as if in great hurry. They knelt together, and Peter prayed. While praying, Peter reached over and laid his hand on Micah's head. After the "Amen" to the prayer, Peter encouraged him to read several passages in the Old Testament of the Holy Bible, especially in the Books of Psalms and Proverbs.

Christmas was most unusual for Micah. For as long as he could remember, he had never experienced such peace of mind. As was her practice, Miss Moodie doubled her servants' rations as present for Christmas. Peter was given two weeks off so that he could attend a religious festival with his village congregation. That meant that Micah had to step in his shoes and perform his duties while he was away. The turn of events motivated and empowered him and enjoyed every bit of the duties.

Chapter 15

"Micah, come here for a minute," Miss Moodie called, the other day. "You really should go and see your father and mother and other relatives before you start attending boarding school in mid-January," she suggested, while looking at him as though anticipating a negative response. Somehow she feared that he would refuse to go home as he had done before. In fact, he had never expressed to her a desire to go. He had never showed any sign of missing home. This had baffled her, and so she thought she should bring it up at this time when the future for him looked so bright. For about a minute, there was an uncomfortable pause during which Micah was fully absorbed in thought.

"What's wrong, Micah? Don't you want to go home for a visit?" she inquired. "It is important that you go," she insisted.

"Thank you very much, Madam. I really want to go. I had been harboring the desire to visit home for a long time. I miss my parents and all my relatives very much," he said with his face showing mixed feelings. "I am only afraid that my father will refuse to let me come back and go to school. He is probably angry with me for being away from home for this long. I am sorry, Madam. Please forgive me. I lied when I said my parents allowed me to work. My mother does not really mind, but my father wants me to stay at home and herd cattle and goats, and help him with other chores. He does not seem to care for education. That is why I hesitate to go home," Micah was almost at the point of crying. "Anyway, Madam I will go. Thank you very much, Madam," he finally said with a rather forced excitement. Miss Moodie gave him some money for the bus fare and other incidentals. A bus home serviced only part of the journey. He would have to walk the rest of the way. She urged him to spend some of the money on presents for his mother and father.

Things were no longer the same at Simon's home. More children had been born to his three wives and new huts had been built. Some of the cattle and goats he knew had been replaced. There were plenty of good crops in the fields, which would make a mockery of the old days when women had to go and beg or engage in barter for food supplies. The rivers were overflowing with water from the recent rains. The never-aging sun was still disappearing in the west behind the mountain around the same time as it used to when he was living at home. There were tall green grass and shrubs everywhere. Indeed, the whole setting seemed more enticing to live at than it did before. Could it have been that absence made Micah's heart grow fodder? Had it not been for the distance from school, would he have minded staying at home this time?

"*Ma-u-u-uya mwanangu!* (Welcome, my son)" his mother exclaimed with tears in her eyes, as Micah appeared from a distance. She dropped onto the ground a heavy bundle of firewood she was carrying on her head and fastened a piece of cloth that was securing her baby onto her back. She approached Micah who was also running towards her. The result was a long embrace and tears streaming from the eyes of mother and child. His other "mothers", Sekwi and Chemwaita, joined in and warmly welcomed Micah back home. The noise aroused a lot of curiosity in several two-year old children who had been born since he was away. Who was this stranger? They must have wondered.

"Where have you been all these years? I heard that you were here and then there working and going to school. I was also told that you have changed your name. Why? What is wrong with the name "Azviperi"? Tell me! What is that European name you have now? Who gave you permission to do all that? Don't tell me your mother allowed you to do that," his father interrogated him before he had said any word of welcome.

"Is that how you greet a child who has been away from home for two years? Don't you have something better to say to welcome him? Have you not been missing him too?" Jay intervened before Micah could even say a word in reply.

"Don't interrupt me, woman. Now I see. You are the one who told my son to go away without my permission. You have done it again.

Who do you think you are in this home?" Simon was furious and threatening to beat her up. There was dead silence in the home while he was shouting all over the place. No child dared say a word; utter a slight sound or even a cough. His other wives intervened and begged him for peace and forgiveness. After all, his child had come back home, they reasoned. The whole uproar seemed to confirm what Micah had been afraid of in his father. Was he going to be allowed to go back to Miss Moodie and then to Rusitu Mission? What if he refused totally to let him go? The thought of that possibility saddened him. He started to regret coming home in the first place. His fears finally vanished when his father calmed down and later apologized for fussing over the issue.

Micah's parents sitting in the forefront

Despite the initial dust at his arrival, it was a great feeling to be back at home. He now had additional brothers, step-brothers, sisters and step-sisters. He had missed his mother's traditional cooking and some African food—sadza, indigenous and locally grown vegetables. He had missed, especially, tender pumpkin leaves cooked together with tender pumpkins all seasoned with home-made spices or fresh cream. He had also missed eating the innards of goats, chickens, and fish caught from the nearby creeks. He had been missing freshly boiled or roasted mealies (corn on the cob), boiled *nzungu* (fresh peanuts) and *nyimo* (round nuts). It was a great feeling to see and enjoy his family again. After he gave his parents the presents he had bought in Melsetter, he recounted to them how his life had been and that his name was now Micah, not Azviperi. His parents' protest to this change of names was mild, as they had to do the same thing to meet the colonial government's requirement for the registration of their marriage.

With excitement, Micah told them everything about Miss Moodie and where he was going to go when school term starts. Jay was exhilarated, but Simon appeared to have some deep reservations about the whole idea of a European taking over the affairs of his child. Why was she doing it? How was he to pay back the money she was spending on him? Would Micah be able to pay back the money? Who gave her permission to employ and educate his child in the first place? What would other people in the village think of him if they heard that a white woman had usurped his parental responsibility over his child? After all the Europeans were oppressing and exploiting the Africans. There was to be on dealing between Africans and the Europeans. To him, Miss Moodie was making a political move with very serious future political consequences for the whole African nation in his native country. Inwardly he pondered the situation and resolved to stop her from interfering with his family. For now he would not disturb the plans and arrangement.

Micah became the center of attraction and entertainment of his siblings and the other local children. For several days, he told them many stories of places he had been to and the experiences he had had. They revered him like he was a gaisa, and he seemed to enjoy the attention he was getting and providing them with some form of entertainment. Soon he began to miss seeing cars and bicycles as well as people in an urban setting, but quickly realized that he would soon go back there and go to school. Before he went, he spent a lot of time visiting his father and asking him about hunting. It was obvious that internally, his father had also been missing his child as well from the way he was telling him about his trips to South Africa and hunting experiences. He had been yearning to see him grow into boyhood and to contribute towards his social maturity by offering him guidance and advice. It was the father's or uncle's traditional role to orient the boy into adolescence, and Simon felt he had been denied of that role since his boys started going to school away from home. He was going to do just that before Micah returned to school.

Chapter 16

A journey to South Africa was perilous and lasted for months as some of the job seekers had to walk from Southern Rhodesia through the Savannah grassland infested with vicious wild animals. A return journey, however, was safe, at least from wild animals, in that the gaisa would have enough money for train fare from Johannesburg to Salisbury. Many stories circulated in the villages about people who went missing on their way to South Africa having been eaten by lions and hyenas, gored by buffalos, trembled by elephants or starved to death while on the way. Simon and other people who had traveled there had narrated several stories about these dangers, and he could name some of the people he knew who had become prey to wild animals. Simon had, on many occasions, strapped himself onto between branches of tall trees at night in order to sleep. With the help of the local villagers, he and others had spent many months circumventing those areas most notorious of such dangers. Those were the hazards involved in traveling to South Africa, all in an effort to find economic means to support one's family.

"Mika (the Shona version for Micah), now that you are growing up and will soon become a man, I want you to remember that a man must learn to fend and protect his family through thick and thin. That is why I chose to leave home, went to South Africa and took the risks of working in dangerous gold mines. I married all my wives, bought these herds of cattle and established this household with the money I earned there," Simon said in a form of lecture.

"Yes, I know father," Micah said politely with his check resting in his left palm. "But the only problem, father, is that most of my brothers and sisters at home here are not going to school," Micah complained.

"But what do you need school for?" his father snapped back looking straight into his son's eyes. Micah did not try to answer that question for he realized that by doing so he would be opening an old wound. An awkward silence descended. Simon finally decided to break the silence by telling his son a story, which happened a long time ago.

One day man called Tafa, and his wife were traveling from one village to another through an isolated area covered with tall dry grass and short trees and shrubs. No villages were in the vicinity. Tafa, armed with a spear, an axe, a machete and a shield, was walking several steps ahead of his wife. His duty as a man was to protect his family by wading off any danger that might arise. His wife was carrying a heavy load of supplies and a baby boy strapped securely on her back. Due to the weight of the baby and the load, she was lagging farther and farther behind her husband. As they were approaching the spot where the grass was thickest, the man did not realize how far behind she was lagging.

A hungry young lioness was lying behind a heavy concentration of grass over a relatively flat ground. As the man approached the spot, the lioness started running towards the man. The man panicked and threw all his weapons in all directions. The lioness leaped in the air and knocked him onto the ground. It securely pinned its prey on the ground, and, before delivering the fatal bites on the man's neck, the lioness raised and turned its head sideways to be sure there was no threat anywhere. When the woman saw what had happened to her husband, she swore to rescue him. She dropped her load, got hold of the lioness' tail and began to tag and pull it vigorously. Surprised by this action, the inexperienced lioness jumped off the man and started swinging in circles in an attempt to free itself from the woman's grip. As soon as the man felt himself free, he got up and started to run for his dear life, leaving his wife struggling with the lioness.

"*Murume wangu, Tafa, usandiseye ndoga kani* (my husband, Tafa, don't leave me alone!) Help Tafa! Come back and help me! Please, come back!" his wife kept on screaming and pleading for help.

Tafa pretended not to hear. He did not even look back to see what was happening to his family. He ran faster and was gone. Seeing that her husband was gone, she kept on tugging and pulling. Thus a battle ensued as the two enemies swung sideways, backwards and forwards over and over again. The lioness got tired and slowed down a little bit.

As it was picking up speed again and increasing the force, the baby on the woman's back began to cry. At the same time the cloth that was securing him on her back was getting loose. The woman held on and kept on tugging and pulling the lioness by the tail and continued screaming for help. The tug of war went on for almost an hour, and both were getting terribly exhausted, but the woman did not dare surrender or let go the tail.

As if by providence, two hunters heard the woman's screams and the baby's cries. They rushed to the woman's aid and killed the lioness. They accompanied her to her village and reported the incident to the village elders who searched for her husband everywhere without success. On the second day, they found him hiding in someone else's barn. The village court charged and found him guilty for abandoning his family in danger and for cowardice. Both the woman's father and the chief of the area fined him for the offense. In addition, he became a laughing stock and an outcast of the village.

Micah's father explained that the story was widely used to teach teenage boys about manhood, bravery and responsibility. He advised his son never to forget it. He added that a man must never run away from his troubles and that it was an honor dying a brave man than a coward. His son intently listened to everything his father had to say, and this helped to reestablish a healthy father-son relationship.

The painful moment soon arrived for him to bid farewell to his family and return to Melsetter. His father unexpectedly did not show resistance towards his leaving nor did he seem excited about it. His mother offered him food supplies for his return journey and wished him well in school. It was hard for him to leave and for other children to see him go away.

He found Miss Moodie worried about him, as the beginning of the school term was now a few days away. She was worried his father might have decided to keep him at home. Although there was nothing she could do about it, she feared for Micah. She knew how desperately Micah wanted to go to school, and therefore to have denied him of that chance would have been unkind. Thus when he showed up late in the afternoon three days before school was to start; her face visibly showed a sign of relief. Upon hearing Micah's voice, when he was talking to Jim and Peter in the kitchen, she unexpectedly and without warning opened the kitchen door. Jim and Peter mechanically stood up showing fear mixed with respect.

"Oh! Micah, you are back. Welcome! How are you?" she said with some unusual excitement. She remained standing at the kitchen door with both hands resting on her hips. Under normal circumstances, she would not come back into the kitchen after instructing Jim what she wanted for lunch and dinner. That way her servants would work without unnecessary interference from her or a feeling that she was watching over their shoulders.

"How are your parents and relatives?" she asked with a grin.

"Thank you, Madam," Micah said standing at attention but with a broad smile.

"They are all well. They said thank you for everything," Micah replied.

"Come and see me soon after breakfast tomorrow," she ordered and quickly disappeared behind the kitchen door.

Micah was tired and hungry. His room was still available, but there were no mealie meal (cornmeal) and other food supplies for him to cook dinner. In fact he no longer had pots and plates. He wondered whether or not he could still eat Miss Moodie's leftover food. Would Jim still let him have some of his cooking? How did he and Peter feel about him feeding on the food they cooked for their Miss? He felt uneasy about the whole situation but did not have an alternative. Should he go in and ask her about it? He wondered. Should he ask them what they felt about it? He did not know what to do.

Hungry and tired as he was, he quietly went straight to his room and took a cold shower. He sat on his crude homemade bed with mattress of dry grass and wondered what to do next about meals. He thought of asking the other servants in the compound for food, but realized they too had just enough rations to last them to the next due date.

"Micah! Micah! Madam wants you," Peter called loudly from half way between Miss Moodie's house and the compound.

Wondering what was wrong; he simply dashed out of his room and ran to the kitchen. She was standing by the outside door of the kitchen facing the compound. He approached her and waited to hear what she wanted to say.

"Oh, I forgot to tell you that Jim will give you something to eat for the next three days. All right?" she asked and hurriedly turned away and disappeared behind the door before he could even say "Thank you, Madam."

Chapter 17

While he was visiting home, Miss Moodie contacted the Reverend John Reeves, the Headmaster of Rusitu Mission boarding school, and Miss Donna, the Administrator of the Mission Station concerning Micah. When Miss Donna heard the name Chinoda, she remembered Micah's brothers who had graduated from the mission. Distantly, she recalled a lady who in deference begged her for help in educating her children. How is it that Micah's name comes up by way of this European lady? She did not sound like she was connected with a church she had heard of nor did she sound like she was a missionary affiliated with a denomination she knew. Both Miss Donna and Rev. Reeves could not understand how an African child got to be in the care of a European.

They wondered what had happened to the colonial government's laws that said there should be no dealings among the Natives and the "superior" Europeans in Southern Rhodesia. What do her neighbors think about her educating an African child who might later become a nationalist revolutionary? There was no doubt that many Europeans had these questions on their minds, and perhaps had tried to talk Miss Moodie out of being what they called a "native—child lover."

The European laws divided the society into different ethnic groups. A small minority of the population was made up of the Europeans or anybody of Caucasian descent at the top, followed by the Coloreds (Africans mixed with white blood), then the Indians. At the bottom of the social ladder were the Africans (the indigenous blacks) who were the majority. Europeans and Africans had separate social services such as healthcare, education, roads and railway system, and the government spent only one-quarter of the total annual budget on the Africans. Christian churches had to step in and fill the gap as much as was possible. They built mission schools, hospitals and clinics. Even residential areas were totally segregated as was the case in South Africa under apartheid laws.

The existence of the Christian churches in Southern Rhodesia was as old as colonialism itself. The denominations, Anglicans, Methodists, Presbyterians, Catholics and others, by agreement among themselves, established mission centers all across the country. The South Africa General Mission, a branch of the Baptists, established the Rusitu Mission in a mountainous eastern region of Southern Rhodesia, about 58 miles southeast of Melsetter.

On Monday, two days before the opening of the school year, Miss Moodie came into the kitchen to instruct Jim what she wanted for lunch and dinner. She seemed to be in great hurry or in bad mood as she totally ignored Peter and Micah who were standing at attention after saying "Good morning, Madam" in unison. Usually, she would answer back by saying "Good morning, Peter. Good morning, Micah. Good morning Jim," with a wide smile, and would then go on and talk to Jim. This time, she just said, "Good morning" once and then went straight to talk to Jim, leaving Peter and Micah wondering what had gone wrong. After she placed her meal order, she dashed out of the kitchen and almost slammed the door behind her, again, leaving her kitchen staff dumbfounded. They just looked at one another, and each one went ahead with his chores. Suddenly, the door opened. Jim, Peter and Micah just froze. Miss Moodie's face appeared, but this time with a surprise smile.

"Micah, come and see me after you are finished," she said and quickly closed the door. It was difficult to read what was going on with her. Micah, in particular was kind of confused and his colleagues, especially Jim, had mixed emotions about the whole thing. Peter seemed less confused and exchanged a smile with Micah. Each one continued with his own chores. Micah seemed to wash dishes, pans and pots in hurry as his mind was on what Miss Moodie had in mind.

She was in her study writing what appeared to be letters, facing the opposite direction of the kitchen. Even though her back was towards Micah, she could see him in the mirror in front of her desk. Micah made an artificial mild coughing sound as he got closer to alert her of his presence. She seemed to ignore him for a few seconds, and then turned around very quickly to face Micah.

"Are you ready to go back to school?" she asked and smiled. Before Micah could reply, she added, "I have sent in money for tuition fees, uniform and other expenses to Rusitu Mission. You will get your pocket money from Miss Donna whenever you need it. Oh, do not be *extravagant*. Do you know what 'extravagant' means? It means being "wasteful, using too much, more than you need," she said without giving him a chance to reply. "I want you to be a good boy. Study hard and aim high. You have a beautiful future, Micah. Do you know that?" she said in a motherly tone resting her left hand on his right shoulder. "Tomorrow, you will take a bus to school. You can come here during some of the holidays, but I want you to go and visit you family as well. You understand?" she added, looking at Micah straight in the eye.

With his palms clasped together, as in prayer, and his head hung on his left shoulder, all Micah could say was "Thank you so much, Madam. I will do my best." He managed a smile before he walked away. He could not believe what was happening. Why was she doing all this? Did he deserve this? How would he pay her back for all this? Micah walked away from Miss Moodie's study as if in a daze. He was overwhelmed with gratitude mixed with some confusion. He went straight to his room in the compound. He knelt down beside his crude bed, closed his eyes and prayed.

"Micah, are you alright in there?" Peter asked knocking on his door. "What did Miss Moodie say? What did she want? He fired several questions while standing at the door waiting for Micah to open it? Micah opened the door and shared with Peter what Miss Moodie had said, and the two knelt down and prayed again.

Later in the afternoon Miss Moodie called him again. "These are for you," she said pointing at a heap of items on the table. "You will be issued with the uniform, shoes and socks at the school," she added. Included on the table were some bed sheets, blankets and toiletries and other supplies, items that Micah had never had in his life. Then she sent Paul, her driver, to the store to buy a medium size metal footlocker. That evening, Micah packed his things ready to go to a boarding school for the first time in his life. The following day, Paul drove him to the bus stop, and he boarded a bus to Rusitu Mission.

Chapter 18

"**N**ew, New'; here we come," a voice burst in song from the back of the bus.

"Today you will sleep in a tree or under the bridge," another bus rider responded in song.

"You will carry out our orders or we will baptize you in water all night," the third voice bellowed in the same song also from the back of the bus.

People on the bus turned their heads to see who was singing. They wondered why they were singing that song and what did they were saying in the song. The song brought a chill down Micah's back. He had heard from his brothers that all freshmen at the mission had to be initiated through hazing for at least four or five weeks. It was a terrible experience for the newcomers, and the school administration seemed unable to stop or prevent it. Micah and a few newcomers on the bus dragged going to school. Micah wished he had been assigned to another non-boarding school, but it was too late. He was already on the bus, almost halfway to Rusitu Mission.

When the bus stopped at the mission, there was chaos as older students who were now veterans of the mission were running from bus to bus and everywhere hunting for newcomers to harass, intimidate and bully. The students who had been singing on the bus Micah was riding on rushed out of the bus, got down their luggage from the top of the bus, and started running about making annoying noises as if they were just wild. Micah and the other new comers just looked at each other. In terror, they remained seated on the bus.

"Is this not your destination, boys?" the conductor of the bus asked. "Get off the bus now and get your belongings from the top of the bus," he ordered "Goodbye and good luck, boys," he added, this time with a chuckle. Did he know what was awaiting all new comers to this mission school?

The boys looked at one another; one of them was visibly shaking with fear. They started crawling out of the bus hoping they would not be noticed by the potential attackers. It was all in vain. They became more noticeable when they got on top of the bus to off-lord their luggage. From that time on, it was a nightmare for all students enrolled in Standard Four. What saved Micah from the ordeal was that he was going into Standard Five which put him in a different category. In addition, a lot of students going into Standards Five and Six knew or had heard stories about his popularly known older brothers who had attended this school. They were famous for protecting new students when they were bullied around during the initiation period.

The boarding master called out a list of new students and assigned to them rooms in the dormitory and read aloud rules related to housekeeping, sleeping arrangements, and meals. Micah was assigned to a dormitory of the Standard Five students. His bed was next to that of Nelson whom Micah's older brother, Chomu, had rescued when he was being beaten up. Chomu had also prevented some bullies from pouring out a bucket of icy-cold water on him while asleep in the middle of the night. To reciprocate, Nelson took Micah under his wings and helped him adjust to boarding life. What a relief and pleasant turn of events.

On Wednesday morning, all students assembled in a three-winged huge church located on the south-side of the mission station. While waiting for church and school authorities, students sang one spiritual chorus after another in accopella, producing waves and waves of beautiful harmony. The church was filled with deafening, but beautiful echoes of boys' and girls' voices in crescendo. When the administrators and staff finally entered the church, all students rose up and stood at attention.

"Good morning, boys and girls," the Reverend Reeves bellowed, his voice echoing in the whole church.

"Good morning, Sir!" the students responded in unison.

"Remain standing until you are told to be seated", Miss Donna ordered.

That was to be the order of the day. Before going to classes, girls would march from their dormitories in twos forming two long lines that snaked downhill towards the church. The boys would do the same and all the students would congregate in the church for one hour of devotion and announcements. Girls and boys would sit in different wings of the church. Staff members would use the other wing, but men and women would sit separately as well.

After the devotion, the Reverend Reeves assigned all students in Standards Four, Five and Six into either A or B stream, depending on their grade point average in the previous year. Those with higher GPA were assigned into the A Stream. Micah was placed in Standard Five (A) class taught by Mr. Sibanda, a well-known disciplinarian but great teacher.

"You are dismissed. Go to your classes," Rev. Reeves ordered.

All students quietly left the church in single files to go their respective classes. Micah was struck by the militaristic culture of the school. Rules were to be obeyed and followed without question. Since the mission was a South Africa General Mission institution, a branch of the Baptist Church institution, it was very conservative and run by Canadian missionaries. Religiously, it was in a way similar to Micah's previous school.

Micah was now in a boarding school. There were no more accommodation, transportation and food problems. How life changed! Clean uniform was required of all students in the mission. Boys wore khaki short pants and short sleeved shirts, grey socks and brown shoes. On Sunday for church, students wore white short sleeved shirt and a blazer. Girls wore blue dresses whose length was to be below the knees and grey sweaters, white socks with black shoes. They had to be clean all the time otherwise one would risk punishment. Keeping one's uniform and bed made up and clean all the time was a challenge to a lot of students, but not that much to Micah for he had learned to do that at Miss Moodie's job.

Peter, the waiter, had taught him how to wash and iron clothes and polish shoes.

The boarding schedule and routine was completely different from the lifestyle he was used to; going to sleep, getting up early in the morning, making up your bed, showering in cold water, going to the dining room for breakfast, washing your plate, and going to class all at the specific time slots. Everybody had to keep time or you risk disciplinary action of the boarding master, Mr. Ziko, nicknamed "Toshororo".

Mr. Ziko was notorious for being very strict and ran the boys' boarding with a Draconian style. Punishment for even minor infraction was severe. So students had to come up with a code of silence or warning signs in order to avoid being caught breaking school rules. If one was in the act of breaking a school rule, and Mr. Ziko was approaching, somebody would either start singing a "Toshororo" song or just shout out the word, "Toshororo".

Micah was mesmerized by the new lifestyle he was now experiencing, except for the food. He had been used to eating some of Miss Moodie's leftover food, now he had to eat mass cooked food consisting of maize (corn) meal porridge with hot tea and a piece of bread for breakfast, sadza with vegetables and, on rare occasions, with a piece of meat in gravy for lunch and dinner. Sometimes the sadza would be poorly cooked, and worms, pieces of an insect or pieces of tiny beetles would be found in the vegetables, and students would protest or go on hunger strike. Students' diet was fortunately supplemented by the fruits. The mission's surroundings were dotted with fruit trees; mangoes, guavas, avocadoes, pineapples and three or four varieties of bananas. These would be placed on the tables at meal time or during break time or after school, students would pick fruits from the nearby trees and plants and enjoy them.

Mr. Sibanda was a medium sized man, light-skinned and rarely wore a smile, to a point of sometimes being scary. In the classroom, he was a challenger and a very stern disciplinarian. As soon as his face appeared at the door, the whole class would stand up and remained motionless. One would hear a pin drop, as he walked to the middle of the room.

"Good morning, class!"

"Good morning, Sir!"

"Sit down!" he would command with a threatening voice.

Micah got scared and began to wonder how he would perform in class and compete with the other students who had been at this mission for Standard Four. But there he was in the classroom facing Mr. Sibanda. His fears were confirmed when it came to mental arithmetic in which the teacher would call out some numbers and students were required to calculate them mentally and come up with answers. One had to think and operate like a mini-calculator. Even though he had memorized the whole12-times table, it was a challenge for him to hold all those numbers and calculate them mentally.

In the whole mission, as was the case at Mhakwe School, everyday, students would enter the classroom first, sit very quietly and wait for the teacher. Students were not allowed to talk without the teacher's permission. They were required to raise a hand for the teacher's attention, and when asking or answering a question, a student had to stand up and talk facing the teacher. No disrespecting the teacher or other students was allowed. In fact, all mission and classroom rules were strictly enforced both in the classroom and in the boarding. It felt like one was in the military academy.

During school vacation, Micah would go and work for Miss Moodie, unless she was out of town. One such vacation, she went to England and arranged for Micah to spend it working for the Assistant Native Commissioner, Mr. Blair, whose house was just a block away from hers. He had two boys, sixteen and twelve years of age. All the African servants, addressed them as "Piknini Baas" (Mini-Boss), and they, in turn, addressed an African servant, regardless of age, as "boy."

"Buya lapa, boy" ("Come here, boy"), a corruption of the Afrikaans language spoken by the Dutch descendants in South Africa, shouted Jack, Mr. Blair's 12-year old.

"Yes, baas," answered their cook running towards him with his hat in his armpits in deference.

He stood motionless, in militaristic attention and with a salute in front of Jack.

"I want my shoes now. Go and get them quickly. Hurry up, Boy!" Jack ordered.

"Yes, Baas," the cook dashed into the house and gave Jack his shoes.

After breakfast the waiter collected the dishes and plates into the kitchen where Micah and the cook were working. Micah was washing the dishes as he had been doing for Miss Moodie. Suddenly the door flank open and Mr. Blair and his 16-year old son came in and went to the bread basket.

"Where is it? Where is that end-piece of bread, heh, boy?" Mr. Blair angrily asked.

The cook and the waited were visibly shaking with fear. Micah stood there frozen and confused.

"What did you do with it, boy?" We want to feed the dog. Where did you put it?" Mr. Blair kept on firing questions.

There was dead silence. The cook and the waiter looked at Micah without saying a word.

"*Yah, Yadya. Yadya*" (corrupt Shona meaning, "Yes, it ate it. It ate it"), Mr. Blair shouted with anger, and while pointing his finger at Micah, accused him of eating it. He addressed Micah as "it", not "he". Was it on purpose, or was it because he did not know the correct Shona word to use when addressing a human being?

Micah almost melted with shame and fear. Miss Moodie always threw the end piece away, or Micah would eat it. He did not know that Mr. Blair preferred feeding his dog with leftover food than feeding a hungry human being. Was he going to report it to Miss Moodie, and what would she feel about him now? The thought of it sent a deep chill down his spine. He did not want to mess up and upset his benefactor. Miss Moodie did not say anything about it when she returned from vacation.

Chapter 19

Standard Six was the final year, and students across the country would take an external examination at the end of the year. Only those who passed in the First Division would be admitted into a competitive and reputable, usually mission academic high school. Those who passed in the Second Division would go to a vocation school, and the rest would fall by the wayside. The following year, Micah was assigned into Miss Hakata's Standard Six A class. He had now become fully adjusted to a boarding life and had been fully prepared in the previous class for this educational level and would need to study extensively for the much dreaded examination. Of course, Miss Hakata was well-known for being a great Standard Six teacher. During the school vacation, Miss Moodie gave him the Student Companion which proved to be an essential resource book. The boarding master required all lights turned off at 10 o'clock and everybody going to sleep. To stay awake longer and study, students had to use flashlights under blankets to avoid being detected and punished. Some would keep their feet dipped in a bucket of cold water to stay awake and study. Micah engaged in some extensive studying and soon knew the information in the Student Companion and in other relevant books from cover to cover.

"Micah, well done! Congratulations!" Miss Moodie yelled out through the window at Micah who was walking down to the compound.

"The Headmaster called. You passed! You passed!" She repeated with great excitement.

The following day, Micah went to the mission to pick up his certificate. He had passed Standard Six in the First Division in English, and the Second Division in Mathematics.

Attending an academic high School or vacation school was the question. Technically, he would qualify for either, but some applications had to be done. The following day after he got back from picking up his certificate, Miss Moodie asked him to see her after breakfast.

"Micah, tomorrow, I want you to go to Umtali. Pack up your things. I will give you a letter to take with you," she said and suddenly disappeared behind the kitchen door.

Peter and Micah looked at each other, and there was silence mixed with apprehension. She had disappeared behind the door before Micah could say or ask anything in response. What was going on? Micah wondered. Did it have to do with school or not? Was she sending him away? Was he to stay there during the school vacation or what? Where? With whom? Why? Was she going to continue to provide for his schooling or not? Was she upset with him for something? But then he remembered the other time she gave him a letter to the headmaster of Mhakwe School. That letter had yielded good results, but this time, it was during the school vacation. He got confused.

Umtali was the third largest city 105 miles away from Melsetter and located near the border with the neighboring country of Mozambique. The following day, she briefly explained to him what she had in mind and what was going on. Micah had packed his school clothes and other personal effects in a trunk. Late in the afternoon, a European couple came to pick him up. He did not know them.

"Micah, here is a letter. Give it to Canon Edward Chipunza of Holy Name Parish in Sakubva Township in Umtali," she said, and gave him a hug for the first time ever.

Micah looked at her, and smiled sheepishly. With mixed emotions, he managed to say, "Thank you very much, Madam." Then, he bid farewell to his colleagues. Peter walked to him, gave him a bear hug and whispered in his right ear, "Bye, bye, Moodie's Boy." They looked at each other almost with teary eyes. Micah turned away and got into the back of the jeep pick up truck enclosed with a tent. What is Umtali like? he wondered. He had never been to a bigger city before, but had heard a lot about crime stories and other happenings of the city life.

As the man was tying the tent on all sides of the truck, Micah requested that part of it be left open so that he could see the surroundings as they drove to the city. Little did he know that it would be pitch dark before long, and that the wind would be unbearable.

The jeep pulled up at the Sakubva Police Station driveway, and the man opened the tent and told Micah to get out. Without saying anything, he just got back into the jeep and simply drove off. Micah stood there. It was now late at night. He looked around. Looked at the highway nearby and saw lights everywhere, but it was quiet for people had gone to sleep. He looked at the envelope and read the name: "Canon Edward Chipunza, Holy Name Parish, Sakubva". Who was Canon Chipunza? Where was Holy Name Parish? How would he find it? How would he get there? He got confused and did not know what to do next.

He looked at the sign in the front of the main police office building that read: "British South Africa Police (BSAP) Sakubva Station." He had heard about the cruelty of the colonial police. People feared the police for their terror on the Africans. Now he was standing in their driveway. It was getting cold and late. He summoned his courage and looked for the office. Because of fear, he hesitated going inside the building.

"Hey, boy, what do you want to report? Did somebody mug you or something?" beamed a deep menacing voice from this husky European police officer.

"I—a-a—am loo-k—iing for this place," Micah said showing him the envelope. His knees were shaking with fear.

"Oh! You see that church across that highway, and the house next to it? That is Holy Name Parish and the priest lives in that house", he said, pointing at it this time with a forced smile.

"Be careful crossing the highway. You hear?" he added with an element of care and concern.

Was he a member of the church somewhere? a Christian? or something? Why a smile now when he found out what his destination was? Micah tried to find answers to these questions.

"Thank you, Sir," Micah said with a salute, for he had seen African police officers saluting a European. He got out of the building and crossed the busy highway.

Between the Church and the house was a big light, but there was no light in the house and no sign of life. More questions came to his mind again. Was there anybody there? What if there was nobody? Where would he go for the night?

Micah knocked on the main door several times each time louder than before, and no one answered his knocks. He paused, and thought about what to do next. He went to the nearest burglar-barred window and knocked two times, and waited for a response. After about three minutes, somebody opened the window slightly creating just enough space for a person to see and speak through it. Through that small crack, a male's voice came.

"*Ndiani?*" (Who is it?).

"*Ndini Micah*" (I am Micah), Micah said, giving him the letter from Miss Moodie.

After about five minutes, the man opened the front door and let Micah in. He introduced himself briefly and offered Micah a couch to sleep on.

Micah could not sleep well, and as a result the night seemed too long for him. Early in the morning, a young woman came out of one of the rooms and walked quietly by without saying a word and went into what looked like a kitchen. She started making noises like she was washing dishes, sweeping or doing something. A little later came out a medium sized man, with light skin complexion.

Thinking that Micah was still asleep, he said with a low and soft voice, "Its time to get up now. Did you sleep well after that long trip?" Without pausing for Micah's response, he continued, "I am Canon Chipunza. I met Miss Moodie at the Cathedral, and she talked to me about you. Welcome to our home."

"Thank you, Reverend," Micah managed a measured response.

He did not know what she talked to him about and the details of what was going to happen from then on. Before long his wife came out and was followed by a little girl from another room. After the introductory formalities and breakfast, Canon Chipunza took Micah to his parsonage office.

"Wow, Micah, what an extraordinary life story I have heard about you. God is truly blessing you. Do you know that?" he asked as he sat in his chair behind a crude desk.

He went into what amounted to be a sermon on God's grace, love and acts of deliverance. He asked Micah how much he had read about Moses' upbringing, Joseph and other major characters in the Bible.

"Here is what we are going to do," the Canon said, and after a brief pause, he continued, as he settled down and rested his elbows on the desk. "The first thing is to find a high school for you for Form I (Grade 9). I have talked with the headmaster of St. Augustine's Anglican Mission for you to attend high school there. But because you are not a member of the Anglican Church and you passed mathematics in the Second Division, the headmaster wants you to take an entrance examination tomorrow. Can you do that? Miss Moodie has made the necessary arrangements to pay for your educational expenses.'

"Yes, Sir. Thank you, Sir." Micah replied.

"No. No. No. Don't address me 'Sir.' Just call me 'Canon', alright? He quickly corrected and patted Micah on his left shoulder.

An entrance examination, again? Micah thought and was reminded of the Mhakwe School situation. To prepare for the examination, he started reading again the Student Companion he had used at Rusitu Mission, but it was strong on English and Social Studies and did not have a good section on mathematics. Besides, there was not much time to prepare anyway. The entrance examination was administered by a European priest who did not seem much welcoming to Micah. Two days later, Canon Chipunza called him in his office.

"Well, the headmaster said you did not do well on the mathematics section of the examination; therefore, he is unable to offer you a place there," Canon Chipunza reported. "We are going to try Hartzell High School at Old Umtali United Methodist Mission. I know the headmaster there. He and I grew up together and we both have farms in Marirangwe south of Salisbury, the capital city," he said with a comforting voice. "Besides, this school accepts qualified United Methodist members and non-members as well, which is good," he added.

"Hello, Edward! Oh! Pardon me; Canon Chipunza! How are you? Haven't seen you in a long time," the headmaster, Mr. Alec Gwanzura greeted with a loud laughing voice. "What brings you here today? It is really nice to see you again", he went on. "And who is here with you, Canon?" he asked.

Obviously, he was a talkative man and did not pause to allow his visitor to respond. After a moment of personal greetings indicative of their long time acquaintance, Canon Chipunza introduced Micah and explained why he brought him there.

"Do you have your certificate with you, Micah?" the headmaster asked.

"Yes, Sir," Micah replied handing it to him. He looked at it briefly and said that was the qualifications he was looking for in the applicants for Form I in his school. He added Micah's name to a long list he had on his desk.

"So, Micah Chinoda, I will see you when school opens in January," he said and quickly shifted attention to his friend and started talking about things pertaining to their farms and various other issues of interest.

Since Micah had never been in a big city, Canon Chipunza introduced him to the city's shopping centers and other places and things of interest. What a different world this was to him. The Chipunza family tended to give Micah some kind of preferential treatment. At the table during meals, they would hand Micah bowls of food and ask him to take some first, before everybody else. This made Micah feel a bit uncomfortable. First, the African custom required adults to take their share of food first and then children. Second, he would not know how much food to take so as to leave enough for others. It was also difficult for him to understand why they were treating him that way.

The Reverend Canon Chipunza and his wife had three grown up sons, three boys and one daughter. The youngest son and fifth child had just completed high school but was not doing anything else. Their grown up daughter was a teacher, had her own daughter and was living with them at the parsonage. During school vacations, he and his family would go and check on their farm. A member of his church would be assigned to make sure the parsonage would not be vandalized while they were gone. From then on, they took Micah with them each time they went, and he helped do some chores at the farm. He never had chance to go back and work for or visit Miss Moodie again. Whenever he was at the farm, he would think about life at her house, and being spoiled while there. He missed it. Could that have been the reason why she handed him over to Canon Chipunza? Did she give in to pressure from Europeans who hated her raising an African who might turn against them when he grows up? Micah wondered.

Chapter 20

The Old Umtali United Methodist Mission itself was surrounded by hills and located 10 miles from the city of Umtali. It had a complex set up made up of a hospital, printing press, elementary, middle and high schools, and several departments of the United Methodist Church. The population was made up of students, teachers and staff with their families. The boarding facilities were only for high school students. Elementary students came from the surrounding farms and homes of the people employed at the mission itself.

Hartzell High School was a highly reputable academic institution which had students of various economic and social backgrounds from all over the country. It was a rival of St. Augustine's Mission High School, about eight miles away and other reputable mission high schools in the country. It was a privilege to be a student at Hartzell High.

The boys' and girls' dormitories were located about a mile apart on different sides of the mission separated by the school buildings and houses. Each was a separate entity and had its own boarding master. The only time boys and girls came together was during classes, functions and church activities.

A day before the opening of the school, Canon Chipunza took Micah downtown and bought him school supplies, including uniforms other necessities. He did not quite figure out how he got the money from Miss Moodie to pay for all these items. On the opening day, he brought Micah to the school and helped him get settled in his dormitory, the first time he had had an adult do that for him. He was surprised to see the number of buses and private vehicles dropping off students. It seemed like the school was more than ten times bigger than Rusitu Mission. Getting settled into a boarding school was not a problem because of his previous experience, besides, there was no initiation of new comers. Old students greeted one another and new students got acquainted with each other.

On the first evening, Mr. William Marima, nicknamed "Chiponda" by students, laid out boarding rules and the consequences for breaking them. He sounded fair, less threatening and approachable. The food was almost the same as that of Rusitu Mission, except there was no abundance of fruits. After breakfast, students went to start attending classes, and Micah blended in well with other students from various areas of the country.

One day when he was now in Form II (10th grade), the headmaster came to his class. As he opened the door, all students rose to their feet and in unison greeted him: "Good morning, Mr. Gwanzura".

"Good morning, class. Be seated," he responded.

The whole class froze. The teacher stopped teaching; students stopped working, and stared at Mr. Gwanzura standing at the door.

"Where is Micah?" he asked. There was a pause as he scouted across the room. Micah raised up his hand from the back of the class.

"Micah, come to my office," he said and disappeared behind the door.

All students and the teacher turned their heads and looked at Micah. The headmaster was not in the habit of calling students to his office unless they were in trouble. Was Micah in trouble? What had he done that the teacher and other students did not know about? They were scared for him. He quietly got out of his seat and slowly walked towards the door. He felt like melting with a mixture of fear and embarrassment. When he got to the office, the headmaster was already seated at his desk facing the door. As Micah walked in the door, he saw the back side of a European's head. It was Miss Moodie sitting in a chair facing the headmaster and away from the door.

"Hello, Micah. How are you?" she asked with a motherly voice and a smile.

"I am very well, thank you, Madam. I am happy to see you. What a pleasant surprise?" Micah replied. He stood at attention until the headmaster offered him a seat.

"I have some papers for you to sign. Sign here," she instructed pointing at a dotted line. He wrote his name on the line.

"Oh! No. No. Sign. Sign in cursive. You know?" she said, and started laughing, and the headmaster joined in the laughter.

Micah signed again, this time in cursive. What were those papers for? She did not explain what they were for, but he had noticed the words: Central Africa Building Society (CABS) at the top of the papers, and *Chinoda Educational Fund* handwritten in capital letters on one of the lines.

"You may back to class," the headmaster said.

"Goodbye, Micah, work hard in school. You hear?" she said with a wide smile betraying some concern and deep affection.

"Thank you very much, Madam," he said and walked out of the office.

She had never displayed that much level of affection before. What was going on? Micah wondered. Perhaps she had been missing seeing him around in her home.

As he was walking back to class something started bothering him. He stopped half way between the office and the classroom. She did not look as healthy as she used to be, he thought to himself. Was she sick? Would he be able to see her again soon? What if she got sick, would he able to visit her? The death of her brother, Brigadier George Moodie, a few years back came to his mind. There was something in the air that did not seem right. What was it? Fear gripped him, but he managed to brush it off his mind and continued walking back to class.

Micah wrote letters to Miss Moodie inquiring about her health. Her cousin, Miss Moore, came from UK had come to stay with her and informed him about her illness.

BERIHILL.
BOX 17.
NELLETTED.
SOUTHERN RHODESIA.
5. 2. 64.

Dear Micah.

Thank you for your
letter. You will be pleased to
know that Madam is getting
better: slowly, but I believe

steadily.

She was pleased to have
your letter and so am I to
learn that your new school is
so fine and that you are to

study so many interesting and
important subjects. You will certainly
have your work cut out to master
them.

If the opportunity occurs, I shall
be delighted to visit your school,
but it may not prove pos-
sible this time.

I hope you are getting on
well and not feeling too much
of a "new boy" — Children, boys
and girls can all be thoughtlessly
unkind to newcomers — When I
first went to school my life was
a burden for my first term — all

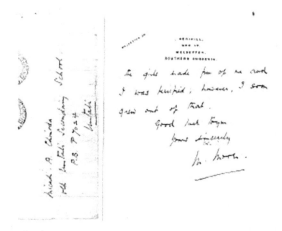

Six months later, Canon Chipunza came to the mission.

"I am looking for Micah. Can you tell me where he is?" he asked Anesu (meaning "God is with us"), one of the students who was walking near the mission store.

"He is practicing hop-step-and-jump over there. He is my dorm mate. I will get him for you," Tafa, another student, said and took off running.

"Micah, a priest is looking for you over there, at the shop," Tafa said with a bit of excitement.

When Micah looked at Canon Chipunza's face, he could tell something was terribly wrong.

"Micah! I am so sorry. Miss Moodie has died. The funeral is tomorrow. I will take you to Melsetter in the morning," he said looking at the ground as if in meditation.

He asked the headmaster and the boarding master to excuse Micah from school for a few days. Then he picked him up and took him to Holy Name Parish. The next day, he drove to Melsetter for the funeral. His wife sat in front and Micah sat in the back. They got to Melsetter almost at the end of the funeral service. But racial problems got in the way. Europeans did not allow Africans to attend their funerals. As a result, Micah and his company were not allowed access to say goodbye to Miss Moodie's remains. Canon Chipunza got upset, and he just angrily ordered, "Let's go back, Micah! Come on! Get in the car!" He drove off. And that was it.

There was silence all the way back. Only Micah's sobs in the back seat could be heard. He was crying uncontrollably.

"Oh, Micah," he tried to break the silence.

"In case you are wondering how you are going to pay for school; don't worry. You must thank God. Remember she left you enough money to complete your education", Canon Chipunza continued trying to comfort and to console him.

"She told me that she came to your school the other day, and you signed some bank papers. I am your guardian now. I have the bank book, and you and I will sign for withdrawals," he added.

That did not seem to help that much. Micah felt horrible and cried all the way back to Umtali, and for several days afterwards. He could not believe that seeing her at his school that day was the last time. Had he known then, he would have perhaps given her a hug or said something more than just "thank you, Madam." If he had had an opportunity to say goodbye to her or to see her being buried, maybe he might have felt better.

(Excerpt from Micah's diary)

In the colonial mission schools, students wore neatly kept and clean uniforms and respected elders and teachers. A student would not speak to his senior with hands in his pockets, and should raise his/her hand to ask or answer a question in class. Talking without being recognized by the teacher was not allowed. When a visitor or teacher entered the classroom, students were to stand at attention and greet the visitor.

"Good morning/afternoon, Sir/Madam," in unison.

Good morning /afternoon class. Be seated," the visitor/teacher would say.

Only then would students sit down and start or continue working.

Even though Micah was becoming a typical high school teenager, he stayed out of trouble all the time. When he was in Form III (11th Grade), however, he let his guards down and got in serious trouble. In his class, students sat in chairs with their decks in front of them. Micah sat directly behind Miriam Kanda. Yes, she was very beautiful, intelligent and elegant. She was wearing a blue uniform dress with a cloth belt around her waist line tied in a bow on the back. He liked Miriam and admired the way she tied her belt. In the middle of the lesson, he got distracted and started to carefully and slowly untie Miriam's belt. He made sure she would not be aware of it and that the other students would not notice what he was doing. He practiced making a bow by tying the belt behind Miriam's chair.

The teacher, Mr. Chimombe, must have noticed or just wanted Miriam to answer a question or say something. He called on her, and as she tried to stand up, Micah's deed came out in the open. The whole class just went berserk. Students were rolling on the floor with laughter, others stood up to see what was happening, but the teacher was furious. He walked to where Miriam was sitting to examine the situation closely. Micah closed his eyes and rested his forehead on the desk.

"Micah, go to the office now! Take this note with you!" the teacher angrily ordered.

Micah had to spend three days after school digging a deep and wide hole for punishment. Some students walked by and laughed at him while he was digging, others felt sorry for him, among them was Miriam herself. A mango fruit tree was planted in that hole. Micah wrote her a letter of apology. She accepted the apology, and they became close friends for the two years they were together at Hartzell. He also apologized to Mr. Chimombe, and before the year was over, he had become his most favorite teacher. From time to time Micah would go to him for advice and guidance on various issues in his life.

Over time, Micah's life at school began to be filled with a lot of activities. He was appointed a prefect and house captain. He became president of the student organization, Scripture Union, member of the school choir, United Methodist Youth Fellowship (UMYF), and held various leadership positions. In sports, he became one of the leading competitors in the hop-step-and-jump and tug-of-war sports activities. In his senior year, he became the school reporter for the United Methodist Newspaper, *Umbowo*, (meaning Testimony). When the UMYF was asked to lead in the church services, Micah would be the main speaker.

During school vacations, Micah continued spending them with Canon Chipunza's family, either at their farm or at Holy Name Parish. Working on the farm was hard, but good for him. He needed to learn the importance of working with the soil and producing one's own food. Among the courses he was taking at school were Agriculture and Carpentry. Developing skills in these courses, as well as in academic courses, were essential in an agrarian society. He found these skills to be very useful at the farm. But during the vacation after the first term in Micah's final year, Form IV (12th Grade), the Chipunza family did not go to the farm, which was unusual because it was the time of harvesting. Canon Chipunza got sick. He sent him a check, but before Micah was able to get to the bank to cash it, one of the deacons of Holy Name Parish came to the school to inform Micah that he had died.

A bus, with church members going to his farm in Marirangwe, would stop by to pick him up the next day. The women on the bus were singing and wailing the entire way pass Salisbury to his burial place.

The pastor of the Old Umtali Mission church, the Rev. David Mudzengerere and elders of the church became highly impressed with Micah's speeches when the UMYF conducted worship services. Would he be a good candidate for church ministry? Would he be interested in becoming a minister? They must have wondered. The pastor called him to his office one day and asked him what career he wanted to pursue after high school. Micah said he did not know. The pastor asked him to consider being a minister as he seemed to have religious convictions and to be a talented speaker.

After the fourth year of high school (Form IV), students had two paths. Those who passed in the upper division would go for Forms V and VI then to the university. Those who passed in the lower division would go for professional training. In Micah's case, indications were that he was tailored for the latter. At first, he was interested in teaching, but what Rev. Mudzengerere had suggested, his participation in various religious activities in the school and his life history all seemed to point at him becoming a preacher rather than a teacher. He wrestled with this thought for quite some time. He would have to make a decision very soon as the final year was drawing to a close. He finally decided to apply for a candidacy in the ministry and be a preacher in the United Methodist Church. The local church approved his application and highly recommended him to the Rhodesia Annual Conference. He was accepted.

By the time he sat for the external Cambridge School Certificate Examination, he was already making arrangements to attend the inter-denominational Epwoth Theological College in Salisbury in January of the coming year.

Chapter 21

Epworth Theological College was located on the outskirts of Salisbury. It was a three-year college accredited by the Central Africa Group of Churches and catered for candidates from any protestant church in Rhodesia. Candidates with the Cambridge School Certificate or the University of London "O" Level diploma would take A Stream courses, and those with the Rhodesia Junior Certificate would take B Stream courses. The sponsoring churches would pay for tuition, books, and food and housing expenses for their candidates plus a stipend to cover their personal incidentals.

By the time the results of the Cambridge School Certificate Examination came out in February, Epworth Theological College had already started. Micah, who had passed in the Lower Division, was already enrolled there.

"Hello! Is that Micah Chinoda?" beamed Mr. Chimombe's voice from the other end of the telephone line.

"Hello! Yes. This is Micah," he replied.

"Yah, this is Chimombe. As you know the results are out and you have been accepted for training at the Umtali Teacher Training College. Are you going?" he asked emphatically.

"No-o. I am already enrolled here. I want to be a minister," Micah replied.

"Now, wait a minute, *Mufana* (Youngman), ministers are not paid well. Do you know that? Plus, there is not much future in the ministry. You are too smart for that! Don't you see? You are being stupid. Go for teaching! Okay?" He continued raising his voice.

"No, Sir. I am happy where I am now. Thank you, though", Micah replied with a sad and rather uncertain voice.

"Okay, but you are being stupid. You know that! Bye!" He banged the phone as he violently hung up.

Micah looked at the voice part of the phone as if it would display Mr. Chimombe's angry face. Was he making the right decision here? Would he regret later for choosing the ministry? Why all the trouble to get an education then? He was deeply troubled, and did not know what to do. "Oh, well. Let it be," he just resigned and never thought of it again. He reasoned to himself that whatever was left of the *Chinoda Educational Fund* would give him a head start in future or "God would provide". Mr. Chimombe and Micah never saw each other again.

Theological and Biblical courses were a challenge to all students partly because of cultural biases and settings they detected in most of the books they were required to read. It could also be because all the professors were missionaries from Europe and United States of America. Very little attention was given to liberation theology relevant to the political situation at the time or to the African culture. Nevertheless, students were kept busy, and the three-year training period went by fast.

Micah paid the required roora and got married to Lucciah Chivunze, and they had their first child. They gave her a Shona name Chemapiwa (meaning: *For that, which you are given*) and Minnah for the middle name, after Miss Moodie. This was a major change in Micah's life. Now he had family responsibilities and college work to do.

When Chemapiwa (Chem for short) was learning to stand up on her own, the Chitiyo family invited them to the afternoon tea and visiting after church. On occasions like that, the hostess took the opportunity to share the use of her most expensive china set and table cloth. She made beautiful tea from the country's most popular tea blend, Tanganda Tea. After drinking tea with biscuits, the two families relaxed and told stories, and were just having lots of fun. Without anybody noticing it, Chem crawled under the table and, within a split of a second, got hold of one corner of the table cloth and pulled to get some support. Everything fell onto the floor and was in pieces. Everybody screamed and gasped. Micah and Lucciah looked at each other in horror and embarrassment. The host and hostess also looked at each other and then looked at their guests. Nobody said a word for a while.

"Oh, no! Please, don't worry. That's what children do," Mrs. Chitiyo managed a smile to try and ease the situation. Chem's parents repeatedly offered to replace their china, but they did not accept the offer.

When Micah was in his second year at Epworth, his oldest sister, SekaAni (*whom are you laughing at?*) was now in Grade Seven, ready for Form I the following year. It was apparent that without financial help, Grade Seven would be terminal for her. So Micah suggested to her and she agreed to become a Roman Catholic nun. Her application was accepted and she joined St Mary's Dominican Convent in Rusape, changed her name to Felistas, and was enrolled for Form I in an all girls' mission secondary school near the convent. All school expenses were to be paid for by the convent.

Towards the end of her second year at the convent and of Form II, the soon to be Sister Felistas visited her home village wearing her nun's uniform. When her father saw her wearing that uniform, he got furious.

"Yes? So, this is what you decided to do? How dare you want to be a nun? Did you, Mika and your mother conspire to do this?"

Her mother did not dare say anything. Felistas did not dare either. They just looked onto the floor.

"Heh? Answer me. Don't just sit there as if you are deaf? Is that what they are teaching you now? You know what it means to be a nun? That means no marriage; which means no lobola for me. No, I can't have it that way. I want you out of that convent, or else—!" he threatened and stormed out of the house. One could hear his feet stamping on the ground as he walked away to his second wife's house.

Felistas and her mother ignored what had happened and was said. At the end of her visit, she returned to the convent, but she just did not seem happy. Something was in the air, and sure enough within two weeks, the administrator of the convent called her to her office.

"Felistas, I am so sorry, child. We just have to let you go. Your father went to the nearest St Patrick's Catholic Mission and complained bitterly against you becoming a nun and attending school here," she said patting Felistas on the shoulders and comforting her. Felistas cried her lungs out all the way to her dorm room to pack up her belongings.

At the end of Tuesday afternoon classes, Micah got to the house only to find Felistas sitting on the sofa crying. He asked why she was crying and not in school. Bedsides, it was towards the end of her last term in Form II.

"I have been dropped out of the convent and school because of Dad", she said uncontrollably sobbing.

Micah consoled her and told her that she was not the only one to whom their father had done this. In fact, he had asked his oldest son, Mwaita, to write a letter for him to Miss Moodie telling her to stop educating his son. Fortunately he refused to write it. Micah then assured Felistas that God would open another door for her. He then enrolled her at a dressmaking institute in Umtali. After graduating, she proved to be a talented and successful dressmaker, running her own shop and supporting her family.

The graduation ceremony at Epworth College was adorned by high ranking church members and leaders, and families of the graduates. Bishop Abel Muzorewa of the United Methodist Church was the guest speaker, and an American missionary, the Rev. Tom Curtis, District Superintendent of the Salisbury District, represented other leaders of the United Methodist church. The principal of the college, the Rev. Eric Eriksson, read the names of the graduates and announced that the valedictorian of the A Stream graduating class was Micah Chinoda. He graduated with an Associate Degree (Diploma) in Theology and Biblical Studies. It was a great honor to be recognized as such, and he delivered the valedictorian speech.

"Congratulations, Micah! You make me and the United Methodist Church proud," Bishop Muzorewa said firmly shaking his hand.

"Thank, you, Bishop," Micah responded with a bow.

Micah and his father after the graduation from Epworth College

Micah's youngest brother, Morgan, and his mother

The Rhodesia Annual Conference of the United Methodist Church held its conference in January, and Micah and the other candidates, who had completed training at Epworth, were ordained as Deacons and given appointments. The Reverend Micah Chinoda was appointed as the District Director of Christian Education in the Salisbury/Bulawayo District with the Rev. Tom Curtis as his District Superintendent.

The church provided his family with a house in Harare, an African township in Salisbury. While serving in this District, the second child was born, and they gave named him *Tendai* (meaning: *Give thanks*) George. When the two children's first names were put together, they expressed the parents' inner feelings of gratitude. Chemapiwa Tendai: *For that, which you are given, give thanks.*

The political situation in the country was becoming worse and worse. The European minority government of Ian Smith was continuing to tighten its grip on the country using intimidation, censorship, detentions and all sorts of human rights violations. The church opposed all these policies. Because of that opposition, church leaders and the church's organs of communication, especially newspapers, *Moto* (meaning "Fire"), for the Roman Catholic Church and Umbowo, for the United Methodist Church, were all targeted for censorship and threats of arrests of their editors. Before the year was over, the editor of Umbowo, Ezekiel Makunike was threatened with arrest and the newspaper itself with banning.

The Church had to do something. The Reverend Micah Chinoda was called to the Rev. Curtis's District office.

"Micah, we have a crisis with our Umbowo newspaper. The Bishop and the Cabinet are thinking of appointing you Editor," Rev. Tom Curtis said. "Would you be willing to take that appointment?" he asked. Micah thought about it for a minute, and then said yes, he would accept appointment. That meant relocating his family to Old Umtali Mission where the mission's printing press was. To open educational opportunities for his brothers and sisters living in the African Reserve home, he decided to take Patrick and Sarah under his wings. He brought them to live with him and his family, and they got enrolled in the mission's elementary school.

In the meantime the Detroit Annual Conference of the United Methodist Church in Michigan was discussing the idea that it was time for the Third World churches to send "missionaries in reverse" to developed countries. After all, churches in Third World countries were growing with lips and bounds compared to those in developed countries. The bishop of the Detroit Conference asked the Rhodesia Conference for a "missionary in-exchange" to spend nine months preaching and speaking to its various church congregations and groups on the work of the church in Rhodesia. His former District Superintendent, Tom Curtis, recommended him for the mission.

Before the end of the year, Bishop Muzorewa and his Cabinet appointed Micah Chinoda to serve in the Detroit Conference.

Chapter 22

THE Reverend Benjamin Whaley, pastor of First United Methodist Church in Bay City, Michigan, was instrumental in and spearheaded the Detroit Conference's decision to ask for a missionary in-exchange from Africa. In his and other church leaders' numerous visits overseas, they had been highly impressed with the work of the church, the spirituality of the people and the rate of growth.

In addition, more and more church members in the United States increasingly wanted to know the fruit of their financial support of the overseas missions and what was going on in these Third World churches. Maybe having an indigenous minister come and interpret the work of the church there within the context of the current social, economic and political conditions would provide them with some additional enlightenment, they thought. It was within that context that Micah was appointed a "missionary in-reverse" to the Detroit Conference.

The Rev. Ben Whaley with Micah just arriving from Africa

Obviously, Micah and his wife could not believe the turn of events in their lives. Was this real? Because the children were still too young and they were taking care of his two siblings, it was not feasible for the whole family to go to America together. Mrs. Lucciah Chinoda had to remain at Old Umtali Mission and look after their two children and his two siblings. That was to be the hardest part for the family.

Micah's itinerary and speaking schedules in the Detroit Conference started in the Saginaw-Bay City District, then Port Huron and Flint Districts respectively. He was overwhelmed by the American culture and the environment, the food, weather and the level of technological advancement, above all by the generosity of the American people. Seeing the draw bridge in operation and snow for the first time mesmerized him beyond words. On one of his tours, he was taken to see the Saginaw Steering Gear factory in October. Micah saw the snow for the first time.

"Micah, come and see snow outside," his tour guides informed him. They rushed outside. He stood there in awe, and then stretched his arms with open palms several times intending to catch snow flakes and examine them closely. But as soon as they fell onto his hands, they melted, to the laughter of his tour guides. Some of the highlights of his stay in Michigan included ice fishing, snowmobile riding, and playing with snow with the children, snowball fights, and building snowmen. Some of the children, especially in the Upper Thumb area of the state, had never seen an African before. Some were hesitant to come close to him, and others satisfied their curiosity by feeling his hair, face and hands, and asking him questions.

"How many times have you been chased by a lion?" some would ask.

"How do you sleep in trees?" others asked.

It was easy to tell that most of their knowledge about Africa was influenced by watching Tarzan movies. Adults and older children were mostly interested in the lives of the people, the culture and economic issues and the work of the church.

Among his surprises was the plight of the American Indians which seemed identical to the sufferings of Africans under European colonialism and imperialism. The existence of ghettoes in Detroit and

Saginaw and other major cities and the "white flight" from inner cities bothered him. How could this be when America was said to be the richest and most powerful country in the world? He wondered. In addition, he had seen and heard about how generous Americans were to the people of the Third World countries and wondered why that generosity did not alleviate these problems.

Conversely, however, and consistent with the American spirit of generosity to people overseas, they donated clothes, money and children toys and helped Micah ship them to his family and other people in need in his home country.

In all churches Micah spoke, they wanted to know about his life background, and were deeply touched by the Moodie story. The evaluation of his ministry in the three districts of the Detroit Conference was a mixed bag. However, the Rev. Ben Whaley became interested in raising funds for Micah and his family to come to America and further their education. His idea was enthusiastically accepted by many churches Micah had preached and spoken; after all, they had been touched by his Moodie's Boy story.

Soon a District committee was formed chaired by Rev. Whaley, and a Conference Advance Special Fund was set up for the Chinoda family. The plan was that the Detroit Conference, through the Advance Special Fund, would be responsible for all educational expenses for his whole family while studying in US and the Board of Global Ministries in New York would take care of the air tickets to and from Rhodesia.

Micah, Ben and Vanessa Whaley at the dinner table

His family and two siblings were overjoyed to see him back home. He had missed the second ordination, therefore the conference held a special ordination ceremony for him. At the Salisbury District Charge Conference, Micah was ordained Elder by Bishop Abel Muzorewa.

He resumed his appointment as editor of the conference church newspaper. The minority government was still keeping an eye on the church and its organs of communication. The July edition of the newspaper that Micah edited after coming back was banned for its editorial entitled" *The Valve That Let the Air Out*". The editorial addressed the British Government Commission's revelation of the Rhodesian minority government's secretive and oppressive tactics, over the African majority, and its human rights violations. Usually when the newspaper was banned, the editor was arrested, but Micah was given a stern warning instead.

The Rev. Whaley wrote to say financial contributions from churches in the three districts were ahead of schedule, and that college applications were now in order. Micah applied to two or three colleges and was accepted for B.A. degree, but he decided to attend Scarritt College for Christian Workers in Nashville Tennessee. His credits from Epworth Theological College were transferred to Scarritt College. Thus, another opportunity in education and the benefits thereof were opening up, not only for him but also for his wife, children, brothers and sisters, and indeed the children of the Chinoda clan, born and the yet-to-be-born.

Chapter 23

For a long time Micah had been subjected to a political situation in which he was barred from meaningfully attending Miss Moodie's funeral or seeing where she was buried. Now the thought of going overseas for a long time without visiting her grave was simply tearing him apart. To make matters worse, one of the many stories his grandmother, Pfupfume, had told him kept on ringing in his ears.

Grandmother Pfupfume

The story was about a vagabond who survived on wild fruits and berries. One day he stumbled upon an oasis of ripe, succulent and enticing fruits. He decided to help himself to the fruits, and as he was just about to reach and pick some, a loud voice came for behind the bushes.

"Hey! You! What are you doing?" a springbok (an animal of deer family) shouted.

The man jumped in terror and started to run.

"Eh, stop! You coward! You thief! Don't you have manners?" the voice echoed.

The man stopped, looked around to see where the voice was coming from.

"Over here. Why are you picking my fruits without asking?" shouted the springbok

"Well, I—I—didn't know somebody owns them," the man replied with a deep sense of guilty. "May I have some, please? I am starving," he begged.

"Yah, okay. Eat as many as you want. Next time mind your manners", the springbok said with a gentle and sympathetic voice.

After they got acquainted, the springbok told the man that he could give him something that would remedy his problems, on condition that he promised something in return.

The man promised to do anything feasible in exchange for the help.

"Here. Take this pumpkin seed and plant it, but here is the condition. Every morning before you do anything else come back to this little bush. You will find me here, and say 'thank you,'" the springbok instructed.

The man pledged, received the seed and left. He planted it, and within a few days the pumpkin plant sprouted, grew into a big vine and started producing pumpkins in abundance. But every morning before doing anything, he kept his pledge and went back to the springbok and said 'thank you.' He started bartering excess pumpkins for chickens, and other domestic animals. He started a family. But as time went on, he progressively became busy and preoccupied. He began to forget his pledge and started to perform his chores first and then go and thanked the springbok. Sometimes he would skip a day or two. After some time, he started sending his son instead. On one of the days, the springbok asked the boy why his father was no longer coming to thank him. The boy replied that he was too busy to visit. After a few days, the boy brought the news that the springbok was sick.

"Oh, well, he is getting too old anyway. I am very busy. I will go and see him later when I find the time," the man brushed the news aside.

On the next visit, the boy found the springbok dead, and reported it. The man did not do anything about it. Suddenly, the man's possessions started disappearing; his animals and family began to die one by one until he became a destitute again.

That story had played havoc in Micah's mind for a long time, and he could no longer wait for a change and the removal of racial barriers. This time, change or no change, he was determined to go and search for Miss Moodie's resting place. Early one morning, he drove to Melsetter.

The Manicaland Provincial Police Station was protected by a spiked metal fence nine feet high with a heavily guarded entrance. It was notorious for police brutality and harsh treatment of political prisoners. Micah, who was wearing a purple clerical shirt and collar, stopped his vehicle outside the gate, and an African constable yelled from inside.

"Who are you? What do you want?"

"I want to see the Chief Inspector."

"Do you have an appointment?"

"No, I don't, but it is important that I see him today."

"The Baas (Boss) does not see ordinary Africans. Can I help you?"

"No. I want to see him. I have to!" Rev. Micah said impatiently.

The police officer disappeared for about five minutes. Suddenly he emerged accompanied by a senior officer who came to the driver's side to interrogate him while the junior office was on guard.

"Okay, Reverend, park your vehicle right there, and follow me," he commanded.

Behind the huge desk was a heavy set European man adorned with badges indicative of his high rank in the police force. He wore a frightening face and did not look at the people coming in the door.

"Give me your ID," he bellowed. Micah placed it on his desk since Europeans avoided physical contact with Africans. He picked it up and looked at it without raising his head.

"Have you been out of the country within the last two years, and, if so, for how long?" he asked.

"Yes, for nine months," Micah replied.

"Where did you go, and for what? A lot of you Africans are going out of the country these days to train as terrorists."

"I went to the United States of America on church assignment".

"Do you have your passport with you?"

"No."

"I need to see it. Go back and get it!" he ordered angrily, and dashed off to another office without even looking at him.

Micah was furious, but powerless to do anything about it. Two days later, he came back with his passport. The Chief Inspector examined it. This time he looked at Micah with a piercing eye from head to toe several times, as if to scare him.

"Okay, what do you want?" he said menacingly.

"I want permission for me to place some flowers on Miss Minnah Sophia Pigot-Moodie's grave."

He gazed at him in disbelief. How could it be? He must have thought. He had never heard of an African asking to place flowers on a European's grave. Besides, the colonial law of the country forbade dealings between the two racial groups.

"You know the law does not allow Kaffirs (the 'N'-word in US) to be or visit European cemetery? Do you want to desecrate that cemetery or something?"

Micah had to plead with him and explained in details his relationship with the late Miss Moodie. The Chief Inspector seemed disgusted to hear what a European had done for an African. In the end, however, he gave Micah a police escort to the cemetery.

She was buried next to her brother. Both graves had granite slabs and headstones indicative of their social and economic status, and their names and military rank titles were beautifully inscribed on them. Micah placed the bouquet, knelt down and mumbled a prayer while tears poured down his cheeks. At last, he saw and thanked her again, although posthumously.

Here lies Minnah Pigot-Moodie. May she rest in peace!

Chapter 24

Arrangements to leave Rhodesia for United States of America were complicated. He had brought Patrick and Sarah to live with him and attend school at the mission. What would happen to them when he went out of the country? Going back to the rural area would certainly mean a quick end to their chances of going further in education. They were still too young for boarding school. Micah had to ask Mr. Sithole, who was the manager of the Printing Press, to allow Patrick to stay in his home while he attended school until he became old enough for boarding. Micah would send him money for fees, uniform and books and other expenses. Mr. Sithole agreed. Unfortunately he could not find a home for Sarah because she was a girl and still too young. She had to go back to the rural village, and soon dropped out of school at the elementary school level.

The flight from Salisbury to US was also long and full of many long layovers. The children experienced some discomfort as they had never traveled by air before, and Tendai, especially raised some serious concerns with his crying.

Arrangements had already been made for accommodation and enrolment into Scarritt College and Watkins Institute, making it easier for the family to settle down and get adjusted to the new environment. The children went to a day care, and the parents attended classes. Two more children were added to the family; a girl named *Mutsa* (meaning: Mercy/Grace) Tasiwei, and a boy named *Danai* (meaning: Love one another) Mika. For six years while studying in Nashville, Micah served as pastor of Beech Grove United Methodist Church.

MICAH CHINODA SCHOLARSHIP NEWS

A Designated Advance Special
of the
Detroit Conference Board of Missions

GREETINGS, CHRISTIAN FRIENDS . . .

MICAH CHINODA

NEWS ABOUT MICAH'S EDUCATION . . .

Cora Goodwin giving Micah a scholarship check while the Rev. Dr. Dogan Williams and members of the Women's Group are watching.

He graduated with a bachelor's degree in Behavioral Sciences from Scarritt College, and a master's degree in Secondary Education from Peabody College for Teachers and a doctoral degree (Ph.D.) in Social Studies Education from Peabody College of Vanderbilt University.

Dr. Peri Chinoda

His wife acquired a GED and an Associate degree from Watkins Institute and Draughons College respectively. Thus, the Rev. Dr. Micah Chinoda became the pioneer in his family who graduated from high school and college, and he established a tradition at Hartzell High and the United States of America which was followed by his family; brothers, nephews and children. Indeed, Hartzell, in particular, soon became the alma mater for the Chinoda family.

In the meantime, Patrick had become old enough for the Hartzell High School boarding and Micah was sending money for his education. However, before he could complete high school there, Micah raised some funds from local churches and individual friends to bring him over to US for further education. He befriended Daisy Taylor of Belmont United Methodist Church and Cora Goodwin of Gordon Memorial United Methodist Church who joined in and helped raise funds to sponsor Patrick.

They took over and brought him under their wings until he graduated from high school and college. In turn, Patrick, with Mrs. Goodwin's support, raised funds to bring his younger brother, Morgan, to US after his graduation from Hartzell High School. Both Patrick and Morgan ended up graduating with master's degrees in engineering, and soon became successful engineers in their respective jobs.

Daisy Taylor talking to Mutsa while Danai is enjoying a ride on her back

Micah and his family went back to their newly independent country of Zimbabwe. A lot had changed and now he could visit Miss Moodie without permission or police escort. Support for his immediate family, the parents and relatives in the rural village became an overwhelming and a daunting task, but knowing how much he had been privileged, that did not matter. What he was doing for his family and relatives solicited some unusual comments from his reserved uncle, Edward Mukazhi. He came to Micah's office one day for a visit and lunch.

Edward Mukazhi and Micah

"You know Micah; I want you to know that people are noticing and proud of you for not forgetting your family and people in the village. You have had a long and successful educational journey, and have come back home. You are a role model to young folks," he said making himself comfortable in a chair.

"I am saying all this to you with "Ndoga" story in mind, he added.

"Have you heard that story?" he asked.

"No; uncle, I haven't heard it. What is it about?" Micah inquired.

"Well," his uncle cleared his throat and started narrating the story.

"In a nearby village, the people felt that their village was lagging behind others in development because they did not have a highly educated person to represent them. They identified Ndoga who was excelling in school but was about to drop because his parents could not afford his education expenses. So everybody, including elderly people sacrificed and brought their financial resources together and sponsored him through high school. Because he was intellectually gifted; a Scottish missionary acquired a scholarship for him to study medicine at the University of Glasgow in Scotland. He got his doctoral degree in medicine (MD) and married a beautiful Scottish lady who had a master's degree in nursing.

"He returned home and opened his own private surgery in Salisbury. He became very wealthy and famous in the whole city. But he abandoned his own family and refused to visit his home village, or support his parents and relatives at home. Ndoga built a mansion, erected a ten-foot Dura wall with a strong corrugated iron gate guarded by two vicious Dobermans. Nobody, even his parents, dared pay him a visit. If his parents dared visit him, they would stay in the servant quarters behind the house. In his prosperity and success, Ndoga forgot what he was before and where he came from. He forgot who made it possible for him to become a doctor.

"We thank you for not forgetting us," his uncle paused, and noticed that Micah was gazing at the ceiling, as if in meditation. There was a long pause; a very long pause. Micah did not understand the real reason for telling him that story. Was it warning, advice, flattery or genuine praise? Whatever it was, Micah broke the silence.

"No, uncle. I would never forget or abandon my family. I would never forget where I came from. I would never forget the people who gave me an opportunity to get an education. Indeed, I am very grateful and deeply indebted to them."

There was a pause, as if they were not sure of what the other was thinking. Micah broke the silence.

"Let's go for lunch, uncle. I am starving," he said, getting out of his chair and heading for the door. His uncle followed closely behind him.

The Chinoda brothers: Morgan, Micah and Patrick

CPSIA information can be obtained
at www.ICGtesting.com
Printed in the USA
LVHW042021290420
654637LV00006B/533